In Search of Competence And Uncommon Sense

By Larry Marxsen

Published by Larry Marxsen

Written by: Larry Marxsen

Edited by: Bruce Marxsen

Cover design: Larry Marxsen

Table Of Contents

In Search Of Competence

Introduction

After hearing some of my sea stories from my nine years in the U. S. Navy, and his knowing of a few of my civilian experiences since then, my brother (who prefers to remain nameless) suggested that I write a book about Leadership. I first rejected that idea as just so much nonsense. After all, who would want to read anything that I have to say, not to mention the fact that I can't write worth a darn.

Because I have an attitude and thought process that has allowed me to progress reasonably far without a college degree (in an environment dominated by college degrees), it is also (unfortunately) an attitude (not the thought process) which has prevented me from going even further, and it is also that very same personality flaw that has encouraged me to perform this most egotistic thing that a person can do.... put my thoughts in a book for others to read... Yeahhh!!! I get to join our philosophical forebears--Socrates, Aristotle, and Plato... Wait--wasn't Plato a cartoon pooch? Scratch Plato... Kinky Friedman... Yeah, that's the ticket--Kinky-freaking-Friedman!!! I can envision it now; Socrates, Aristotle,

Kinky and me, the officers of philosophers, residing shoulder to shoulder on the Mount Rushmore of great thinkers... Ohhh yeahhh!!!

Uh--anyway, I only finally agreed to put my thoughts in a book as a result of the encouragement of family members so that I could lay the blame on them in the event it is a monumental flop. Also my brother (who wishes to remain nameless) agreed to take the rough edges out of the book, and remove about a gazillion commas (I do so love comma's--and semi-colons, semi-colons are neat too, and I feel periods are really too precious a thing to waste). Remember also that if there is anything that ticks you off in this book--it's my brothers' fault because this was all his idea.

My thoughts in this book will be limited to what I have observed regarding leadership, which is basically competence--supported by Strategic Thinking, Analytical Thinking, and Ethical Thinking. All of which, when utilized properly, are interdependent. Not only is it a blueprint for those who want to be good leaders, but also it can be a guide for those who prefer to be followers that will enable them to choose good leaders to follow.

From an email from my brother (who wishes to remain nameless): With regard to the book--I am editing it from the perspective that you are a veteran with a PhD in life and you have lessons from that life others can benefit from. Your stories sell the point that you have been there, done that, and got the t-shirt. I am trying to get away from any perspective that you have an agenda, except to help those who do not have your experience. That means young and old, stupid and not stupid, leaders/followers, officers/enlisted....

With that in mind, I can pretty much promise that, by the time you finish this book, you will likely discover something that you hadn't known before.

Oh, yeah, be forewarned; I love quotes and anecdotes. Anecdotes are great word pictures for illustrating my points; and quotes offer an excellent opportunity for me to piggyback on someone else's credibility and intellect, not to mention the fact that they sound mucho better than anything that could possibly originate with me.

As a way to establish some small level of credibility, let me give you a short (although, you probably will decide not short enough) biography of my experience.

Chapter 1

Who I am, and where I came from

My first attempt at college was a disaster, I excelled in my major, which was **'Party time--and the deleterious effects of excessive amounts of alcohol on brain cells'**, but my grades were an unmitigated disaster. They were really--**really** bad.

After two semesters of partying and very little in the way of grades or knowledge to show for it I quit. Actually I was asked to leave. Well, not exactly asked to leave, I was not allowed to come back after the semester break. I was just shy of age nineteen by a couple of months and with the military draft looking for cannon fodder in Viet Nam I enlisted in the U.S. Navy in 1968. Since I didn't have the connections (like a future President of the United States did) to get into the National Guard or Reserves; I thought it was my only option. My first couple of years in the Navy was spent in SONAR and ASROC Fire Control (computer) schools, which I really enjoyed.

After nine years and a couple of trips to Viet Nam, among other garden spots of the Pacific, I was discharged after having made it to the Chief Petty Officers Selection Board in just six months over the minimum amount of time. By the way, the reason for that six-month delay was because of a run-in with one of my division officers on the Destroyer, U.S.S. Theodore E. Chandler DD717, I had been assigned to. That run-in resulted in a poor review because of my disdain for **"officers and gentlemen"**. Our differences centered on him accusing me of lacking tact and me accusing him of being, uh, less than a marginal performer (only, I voiced it in much cruder and ruder sailor-speak). I was, after all only a semi-sentient, non-refined enlisted man, and I had our high tradition and reputation of the United States Navy to uphold. During my last two years on the Destroyer I was assigned a few duties that were normally held by a commissioned officer, even though I was just a Second Class, and finally a First Class Petty Officer. At the last duty station that I was assigned to (Fleet Anti-Submarine Warfare Training Center), I supervised the maintenance and operations of about ten electronics labs and simulators. There my division officer and department head were prepared to recommend me for a commission.

Just prior to leaving the Navy I had interviewed for (and was offered) two jobs; the first was with McDonnell Douglas as an instructor to foreign militaries (at their locations) on their missile system (Harpoon, if I remember right), and the second was with a company that provided remotely piloted submersibles and operators to off shore drilling platforms.

Since I had no desire to train people in Iran (pre-revolution), South Korea, or any of the other less than idyllic spots in the world I declined. Also I had no desire to spend a significant portion of my life on offshore drilling rigs.

Upon leaving the Navy I went to work for GTE Information Systems, in Anaheim, CA (which produced mini-computers for stock brokerages and point of sale terminals for fast food restaurants) as an electronics technician. In just over one year I was promoted twice: first to Senior Technician, and then to that of Test Department Manager, whose department consisted of fifty technicians on two shifts. When the General Manager asked one of our supervisors (whom I leapfrogged) what he thought of my being promoted, the supervisor said, *"Fine, except you'll be losing your best technician."* To which, the G. M. responded, *"No, we'll be gaining fifty more just like him."* After six months of improving department output more than 300% with only a 15% increase in payroll, I took over the "Repair and Refurb" facility a few blocks away. Around that same time my name was forwarded to the Chairman of the Board of GTE as being the person to contact in our business unit if anything came up over the upcoming holidays. This was both a tremendous source of pride, and the beginning of my demise at GTE. Since I was a newbie to corporate politics, and had (and still have) a strong disdain for politics and the slime-balls who practice it (both in business, and in government), I ignored what was going on (politically) around me and focused on the work at hand. The long knives came out, and I started experiencing constant sharp pains in my back. As a result I quit and went to work as a Senior Technician for an ex-boss (the man who I had replaced as Test Manager) who had gone to another electronics company in Pomona, CA. The company he was with produced automated test equipment for the electronics industry. Within one year of my leaving GTE, that business unit ceased operations. Their decline was not so related to my departure, but more related to them not having a real business strategy or vision. The result was no future products and a declining market.

During this same time I made my second attempt at college. This trial lasted a few semesters, and consisted of taking a full load of courses at night, while I worked full time (ten to eleven hours) during the day. I got good grades (3.8 GPA) and made the Deans' list, but was soon bored with the slow pace of college courses and disenchanted with the mediocre quality of some of the professors. I completed the coursework for a couple of programming classes in less than two weeks and got 4.0's, but quit one physics class because the professor was wrong about something and wouldn't admit it. I decided that I could learn more on my own, and faster to boot. Uh, did I mention that I have a **large ego**?

I started work at this automated test equipment company as a technician. After designing a couple of pieces of in-house test equipment and training a few technicians, I was transferred to our Chicago sales office in order to work as a Field Engineer covering the central U.S. and Canada. During my two years as a field engineer I inherited other territories as other field engineers quit or were let go, and ended up with the entire U.S., Canada, and Puerto Rico as my territory. I also periodically went to the home plant in Pomona, Ca. to debug engineering prototypes and recommend engineering design changes, as well as developing and conducting training classes for all our customers' technicians as well as our own techs. Shortly before leaving this company I designed a new piece of automatic test equipment that the company decided to produce and sell. Well, I didn't actually design it. The concept was mine, and I showed engineering how to design it. After two years of field service I decided I wanted to give sales a try. I was offered a sales engineer position at both that company and with Schlumberger... I chose Schlumberger.

I was one of four people hired by Schlumberger as part of a fast-track training program for corporate management, and spent two years selling their automated test equipment (costing $35K to $150K per unit) to fortune 500 companies. During this time I helped design (again, I showed engineering how to design) another piece of test equipment, similar to the one at my last company. This they then put into production. While at Schlumberger I went through extensive training (by Holden Corporation) in power based selling and strategic selling (both of which were extremely valuable) and was promoted to a Sales Manager position. I left after two years mainly because I was at odds with upper management over their wish for me to utilize a 'Scorched Earth' strategy (more on that, later) with customers that had decided to buy from the competition. That refusal later proved to be the right choice. All four of us 'fast trackers' were gone within three to four years of our hiring, and Schlumbergers' Automated Test Equipment business unit departed the U.S. within another 5 five years, because of corporate management not understanding: (1) the technology, and (2) the U.S. market. Their business strategy was entirely incompatible with those elements.

I then started my own Independent Sales Rep. Company (with Schlumberger as my first client) on a shoestring. I greatly underestimated the cash needed to last the first year of business; I thought I had found a short cut. I was sooo wrong!!! Only after my decision to kill off the company due to slow cash flow, did the money start coming in. As they say, the operation was a success…. but the patient died.

It was the wrong strategy due to my ego getting in the way, and insufficient knowledge of what I was getting into.

Over the next seven years I went on to a succession of automatic test equipment companies chasing titles (to feed my ego) such as Regional Sales Manager, National Sales Manager, and Vice President of Sales. All of these companies were looking for a miracle worker, and unfortunately I couldn't walk on water. Their business strategies were all flawed (for a variety of reasons). All but one of those companies was out of business within one year of my departure, and one of those companies nearly bankrupted me.

A publishing company that published trade journals and produced trade shows then hired me as a salesman, and within one year I was promoted to National Sales Manager of the High Tech Group… Notice the pattern here? It was during this time that I discovered yet another flaw in my personality. I had absolutely no interest in political correctness, and was (and still am) insensitive to others phobias, wishes and desires. One time I was called into Human Resources and was told that I was intimidating. *"Uh-huh! And?"* That's a bad thing, I was told. I countered that it is, however, a very efficient way of dealing with idiots. By the expression on the Human Resources Manager's face, I was 'speaking in tongue (I have encountered that expression quite often). After about another six months politics reared its ugly head again, and because of that, coupled with a disagreement (and fallout) over business strategies, I departed. I learned that while intimidation works very well on us "Neanderthals" in the Military, it doesn't work very well in civilian life. Thanks to lawyers and do-gooders, there is prescience from Mathew 5 verse 5; the meek have indeed, inherited the earth.

Now, by this time I was pretty much burned out on both sales and management, and wanted to do something that wouldn't contribute to my thriving ulcers and increasing dependence on Zantac. That was when I remembered making a sales presentation to a GM plant a number of years earlier. During a plant tour there I was introduced to a production line worker who had a PHD in Math (he was a local celebrity). When I asked him why in the world would a person with a PHD in Mathematics be putting lug nuts on cars? He looked at me incredulously, like it should be obvious, and his response was simple. *"Because no one can tell me what to think about."* That statement stuck with me over the years, and led to my final choice in careers… truck driving!!! No kidding… While I didn't care much for the long absences from home, the dealing with car drivers who thought driving was so easy they didn't have to pay attention to what they were doing was no picnic, and certainly conversations with most (but, not all) of the other truck drivers was anything but sterling, the pay was adequate for my needs. While driving I could think about anything, design anything, or delve into any social or economic puzzles I wished. For me it was almost the perfect job. The only job that could have been more desirable to me would have been as a sheepherder on a mountain. Unfortunately, the problem was that sheep herding does not pay well. Also, I suspect there isn't even any need for sheepherders anymore. *(What a shame, maybe the world's greatest thinkers for our future could come out of the sheep herding industry.)*. In any case, as an added bonus I had no more ulcers. Now that I think about it, maybe the oilrig job wouldn't have been too bad.

When I was at my next to last trucking-company employer, the owner had not renegotiated the expired contract we were operating under. He said he would just continue under the conditions of the old contract. Well, the shipper had other ideas. Without a contract in force, they started abusing the relationship. When I asked him why we don't negotiate a new contract with better terms he told me he didn't know how. So, I went with his wife (she was the brains in the company) to a meeting to negotiate a new contract. When we concluded the meeting, the owner of the company we hauled for asked me, *"What on earth did you do before you drove trucks?"* So I gave him a much-abbreviated version of this, and then we departed. A couple of days later my trucking company boss called me, and the first thing that he said was, *"When are you leaving?"* I said, *"I'm not planning to leave. Why?"* He said that our shipper was going to offer me a job. I told him not to worry, because the last thing I wanted to do was to go back into an office and work with a bunch of bosses and butt-heads that didn't know what they were doing (or who wanted to do me harm). My boss later told me because of the new contract, this was the first time that he was actually making a profit.

After fifteen peaceful years driving trucks for four or five different companies, and experiencing steadily worsening osteoarthritis, diabetes, and finally, congestive heart failure, I decided to stay home and annoy my wife. That is yet another thing I discovered that I do really--**REALLY**--well.

There is a common thread here. I am impatient, absolutely intolerant of stupidity, refuse to participate in any kind of corporate intrigue, or promote anything that isn't true, safe, legal, ethical or moral (at least, my version of moral), and couldn't care less about being politically correct. Because of my rigidity I have been unable to reach my full potential. I have been true to these core beliefs, and as a result, I have enjoyed reasonable (though not necessarily spectacular) success. I have, at the same time, had no trouble looking at myself in the mirror, or sleeping at nights. Well, except for one hot summer night in Slidell, LA, where I had to spend a humid, smelly night in a truck stop parked between a truck loaded with fish on one side, and a livestock hauler on the other (pheww… that sucked!). Also, because of my Holden training in strategic selling, my fascination with the wisdom of Sun Tzu, as well as my deep interest in war and battle strategy (and tactics), I have been able to come to understand the makeup (and design) of successful strategies and tactics, and how they come into play in everyday life. Ah-ha--you say!!! You may have already noticed my many references to bad strategies by my former bosses. That is because probably the single biggest factor in Leadership and competence is the successful use of strategies (more on that in a later chapter) and is not the rants of a bitter old ex-salesman.

Note: Let me be clear about one thing. I **never** sought promotions because I wanted to be the "Boss". I sought promotions because every step up the chain of command, or organization chart, was one less level of idiots that could screw up my (or anyone else's) life. I guess you could say it was strictly self-defense, or **self-preservation promotions**.

One last thing; I occasionally do not follow my own advice (yet another flaw among many).

Now, unless I have thoroughly bored you and caused you to stop reading this, let's get on with my observations and what I have learned about--**Leadership**.

Chapter 1

Leadership

Throughout my adult life, I have been told by nearly all of my supervisors I am a natural leader, and if I would only channel that ability and be a team player I would really be able to shine. I knew what they really wanted. They wanted me to use this "ability" to lead the people who trusted me. But, like a 'Judas goat', along with leading people--management (or Brass) wanted me to follow them without regard to whether that direction was safe, moral, ethical, legal, or even correct.

During all this time I examined what makes a leader, how it applies to me, and why I haven't used this ability to it's fullest.

First let me say what the dictionary has to say about leadership:

(1) The position or guidance of a leader.

(2) The ability to lead.

(3) The leaders of a group.

Now, notice that there is no statement of right, correctness, legality, morality or ethics. Just as the concept of "capitalism" is an amoral (notice I did not use the term immoral) tool or process, so is the term "leadership". Both leadership and capitalism gain their moral or immoral characteristics from the people practicing them. A leader can lead his or her followers in any direction he or she (see how politically correct I am now?) chooses; good or bad, right or wrong. Hitler was as much a leader as Gandhi was.

I have come to the opinion that there are three kinds of "natural leaders" (without regard to quality):

(1) Those who are leaders because of competence.

(2) Those who are leaders because of charisma.

(3) Those who are 'leaders designated by law'.

People are drawn to follow either the Competent or the Charismatic for similar reasons; trust. People are **forced** to follow the 'leaders' designated by law.

The seat of the chair called leadership is competence.

People naturally seek out those who are competent first and foremost. They wish to follow and put their trust in those who appear to know what they are doing, or what they are talking about. They **trust** they won't be misled. The reason for this is competent people usually tend to be (when possible) accurate, correct, ethical, safe, and legal. Competent people do not usually allow ideology or agenda to excessively influence their position. However, very few people can be completely uninfluenced by ideology or agenda. With that in mind it is understandable why truly competent people are an extremely rare commodity.

For the most part, a competent person tries not to "spin", or trust in "spin". Much like what a Magician does with an audience, the purpose of "spinning" is to misdirect the attention (or focus) of those who may not have a good understanding of what is about to happen. Unfortunately nearly everything one hears on TV, reads on the Internet, or hears from advisors, is "spin" derived from things taken out of context, is based on hyperbole, or is anecdotal rather than empirical evidence. Politicians love to "spin". Probably the best of the five basic strategies that I will cover in the next chapter is the "indirect" strategy. It is a very good and useful strategy, but when used in a less than truthful manner is just another form of 'spin'.

Here is a good place to remind everyone of some definitions. A good example of 'anecdotal evidence' is when someone touts vitamin C as a supplement that can prevent, or even cure flu, colds, viruses and even AIDs. They recount how some people have taken vitamin C and subsequently either didn't contract those diseases or were even cured outright. They will ignore stories about how some people also took vitamin C prior to contracting those diseases, or are in remission from the condition/disease not related to taking them. Whereas, an example of 'empirical evidence' is when a non-biased laboratory does an extensive and exhaustive test or study, and determines that vitamin C supplements have no significant effect on those conditions or diseases. An example of 'hyperbole' (when used as 'spin') is when some people who opposing tax increases refer to a proposed tax rate increase from 10% to 12% as a 20% tax increase (it is indeed a 20% increase), or those favoring to tax increase refer to it as an increase of only 2% (which is also only a 2% increase). Both statements are mathematically correct from two different perspectives, but they are used in hyperbolic terms designed to either scare or placate someone, depending on their ideology or agenda. Of course, I wouldn't want to leave out of the examples of hyperbole the sound bites of the mathematically challenged athletes saying they give 150% effort. Uh, for those of you who are, yourselves, mathematically challenged, giving more than 100% effort is not possible.

I once heard an oil company mouthpiece, explain why oil companies need government subsidies, saying their profit margins are lower than most other companies, and if the subsidies were removed, the price of gas would have to go up in order to make up for the loss. What he didn't say is that gasoline doesn't take a year to make and sell, but it brings back every dollar (with a small profit) within a few days or weeks to be reinvested (compounded). When you Invest $1, and get back $1.10 within 1 day to be reinvested, after 10 days you have $2.59 for a profit of 159% on the original $1 that was invested, plus future revenue and profit being readily reinvested (compounding). Instead of a 159 % profit on that dollar, they choose to "spin" it as each individual reinvestment being unique, resulting in a profit of only $0.10, or "only" 10%. Both are 'spin', and both are mathematically accurate, while each gives an entirely different perspective. A truly competent person sees through the "spin".

Nothing in the world is more dangerous than sincere ignorance and conscientious stupidity-- **Dr. Martin Luther King, Jr.**

*Ignorance is a (hopefully) temporary intellectual condition. Stupidity is both permanent and irreversible—***Me.**

A person's competence is usually limited to the subjects, which they truly know about. Their competence regarding other subjects is enhanced by a willingness to listen to (and learn from) others. A competent person sees through agendas, ideology, and 'spin'. One thing to keep in mind is someone who is standing up and shouting, *"Listen to me,"* or *"Trust me,"* is probably not worth listening to, nor speaking the truth. That person is more likely pushing an agenda. People who don't 'spin', or don't try to

27

forward an agenda, rarely stand up and make noise.

To get back on subject, a large percentage of corporate managers fall into the "Competent" category. But if they were all competent, General Motors, Chrysler, and the Investment Banks wouldn't have needed to be bailed out. If all corporate leaders were competent once leading companies such as Univac, Control Data, DEC, Data General, Wang, Compaq, American Motors, Montgomery Wards, and K Mart would still be in existence. Look what happened to Apple when they first replaced Steven Jobs with the bonehead from Pepsi (at least I think it was Pepsi); it nearly killed the company. After they brought Jobs back to rescue the company, they went on to become once again one of the largest and most prosperous companies in the world.

In the military we see examples of 'competent' type of leaders in Generals Omar Bradley, Eisenhower, and Powell.

With charisma, leaders often rely on the force of their perceived sense of caring and involvement to draw people to them. These charismatic characteristics can be something as silly as appearance, but can be something else such as occupation, wealth, speaking ability, or the seemingly warmth of their personality. These are the people who, when at a party, always have a crowd of people around them. People may be attracted to them because of their looks, their witty repartee, and the way they tell jokes, stories, or whatever gives the follower warmth and desire to be around the 'leader'. Charismatics sometimes take advantage of their position to promote an agenda. If they are knowledgeable and honest, so much the better because it makes following someone a lot more pleasant if you like them as well as respect them. But, if they are using their position to forward a position that isn't necessarily a good idea then they can be dangerous. An example of this is when an actor, or actress, or whacked out rock star, promotes an agenda or something else which they have no extraordinary knowledge or experience. For the most part the "Talking Heads" on TV fall into this category; pretty face--pretty speech--and an empty head. The reason they sound so good is because the empty space between their ears makes for an excellent resonating chamber.

Charismatics tend to be narcissistic (why not love themselves, everyone else does). Although, this is not a universal characteristic, it is an unfortunate flaw in some. Some believe they know what is best for others because they strongly and intimately believe they just know what is best.

In the absence of competence people will follow a charismatic because they are attracted to them with hope they will not be led astray. Politicians tend to fall into the charismatic category, which explains why we are in a near perpetual state of dissatisfaction with the political leaders in our country. We play "crack the whip" with our elections, going from one extreme to another in search of someone (anyone) who will do us no harm.

A person can be both competent and charismatic. When that happens you can have excellence in leadership. These people not only build trust within us, but they can also inspire us. Examples of these are statesmen like George Washington, Winston Churchill, Teddy Roosevelt, and John Kennedy; Generals Patton and Mac Arthur; and certainly, Abraham Lincoln, although I suspect Lincoln's charisma stemmed more from his intellect and orating ability than from his legendary good looks.

The third category of leaders is the law-mandated kind such as Monarchs, Dictators, and the Junior Officers in the military.

You notice I included junior officers and not senior officers. While all officers receive their commissions from congress by nature of having a college degree and military leadership courses with absolutely no regard to aptitude or competence, senior officers are, for the most part, promoted to their ranks on competence. To be a junior officer one does not need a degree in aeronautics, naval architecture, war strategies, etc.; a degree in Renaissance Art will do just fine. These people automatically get placed in positions of leadership over people who usually have much more experience regarding their units' needs, tasks and skills, as long as they have a college degree that indicates they know a "Iambic Pentameter" is not a five-function meter for measuring cosmic rays (it's not, look it up). Because of the long weeding out process to progress to senior officer, most of the incompetent idiots in the junior officer ranks get weeded out, and competence eventually (for the most part) prevails. I know I am being very hard on officers, and in truth, of the dozens of junior officers I encountered, a few were good, most were mediocre, and some were absolute morons. Think "frat boys" playing soldier. Since peoples' lives and well being hang in the balance, this practice can have lethal outcomes. In Viet Nam the worst offenders were occasionaly "fragged" by their own people in self-defense. In my not-so-humble opinion the military would be much better off if they would make everyone start life as an enlisted. They could still promote only people with degrees if that is what is best, but to my way of thinking only competent people would be promoted to the officer ranks because the vetting process would be accomplished at the enlisted level where they can do the least damage.

I am now going to relate a few of my personal experiences while I served nine years in the U.S. Navy (as an enlisted man) to illustrate situations caused by congressionally mandated incompetence. In other words, it was leadership that was neither earned nor deserved, but assigned.

1. We were holding a fire drill in port, while tied to the pier, and I was in charge of the fire team to keep the ASROC

Launcher (with eight-12 3/4 inch diameter solid fuel rocket motors, six homing torpedoes, and two nuclear depth charges) from overheating, catching fire, and cooking off (not a good thing). It can be done, but it required a MINIMUM of two-3 1/2-inch hoses and two-2-inch hoses (if I remember correctly) constantly streaming cold seawater on the launcher. I had been battling with the junior officers about this for a couple of months, because we only had three-2-inch hoses. But, they did not want to call the attention of their superiors to the fact we were not in a good state of readiness. Well, one day when the fire drill alarm went off I went out and stood on the pier instead of on the ASROC deck--supervising. The XO yelled at me, *"What do you think you're doing, Petty Officer Marxsen?"* I yelled back, that *"I abandoned ship in order to save my life, and everyone else still on the ship is dead."*

We soon got our needed hoses...

In the interest of accuracy, I need to point out that the nukes would not explode because of fire, or anything else short of a very specific and controlled chain of events. I just mentioned them to peak your interest. It was the rocket motors and torpedo warheads that were the real danger (big time).

2. Another time, while off the coast of Viet Nam, we were providing Gun Fire Support (GFS) for the "ground-pounders", and I was acting Gun Control Officer. When you have a gun mission they tell you how many guns, which guns, range and

bearing, and how many rounds they want you to shoot for spotting, and how many rounds they want you to shoot for effect. I would then aim the guns, and instruct the gun crews and magazine crews to load the correct number of powder canisters and rounds into the appropriate mount. An example would be when I would speak into the sound powered net. *"Mount one, Gun Control, prepare for two guns 12 rounds HICAP".* When they had them in position and ready, they would say, *"Gun Control, Mount one, twelve rounds ready."*

One of the things you have to keep track of when firing the guns was the number of times fired for each gun in any rolling hour. This information was needed because we needed to know if we had a "hot gun" (fifty rounds in one hour). This was important for two reasons: first, a hot guns' bore wears at a greatly accelerated rate (which results in the need to replace a very expensive barrel), and the second reason is if you leave a round in the breech of a hot gun it WILL cook off (explode), damaging the gun and killing the crew in the mount. We frequently worked with a hot gun (after all, this WAS a war-- uh, excuse me--conflict). Another thing to remember is that you NEVER unload a hot gun. It could explode at any time, and with the breech open that would be catastrophic. You also should not have the hatches going from the mount down to the magazines open because any accident could ignite the magazine resulting in catastrophic consequences.

In this instance, our hatches were open because the transfer elevators to move rounds from the magazine to the mount were inoperable. Guess what, we also had a hot gun.

This is a good time to point out that I not only supervised the guns, but also actually fired them. This was done by placing my hand on what looked like an old Colt 45 Peacemaker handle (attached to the fire control computer) and squeezing the trigger after first sounding the alarms.

So, this time I gave the order to prepare mount one with twelve rounds of HICAP. When *"loaded"*, I then announced to everyone on the net (Combat, Bridge, and Mounts and Magazine) to *"Stand-by,"* followed by two beeps of the alarm, followed by squeezing the trigger, and a very loud boom and ship-lurch. Then the gun mount crew would put the next round and powder canister in the gun, and say, *"Loaded"*, and I would again say, *"Stand by"*, beep the alarm and fire. This sequence was repeated every time we fired a round.

After the twelve rounds had been fired I was about to announce to Combat and Bridge that the guns were empty-- twelve rounds complete, when over the net I heard, ***"Loaded"***.

I said, *"Say again"*?

"Mount one Loaded".

I said, *"We already fired the twelve rounds"*.

"Well, we're loaded, anyway." **Someone in the gun mount had miscounted.**

I said, *"Wait one… Bridge, Gun Control, We have a "hot gun" with a round loaded, request permission to shoot."* (You never say fire aboard a ship unless there is a real fire.)

"Gun Control, Bridge, wait one".

After about 30 seconds, I said, *"Bridge, Gun Control, I repeat, we have a hot gun with a round about to cook off. The hatches are open all the way to the magazine because the elevators are in-op. Request permission to shoot so we don't blow up the ship and kill everyone on board."*

"Wait one." Same thing.

After waiting another 60 seconds, I said to those in Gun Control, *' the hell with this".* Then I announced over the sound powered net, *"Stand-by,"* beeped twice, and fired the guns.

About four or five minutes later, the Captain, XO, Combat Officer, Weapons Officer, and my ASW Division Officer came screaming into Gun Control/Plot.

The Captain yelled, *"Who the hell gave you permission to fire the guns"?*

I said, *"No one, Cap'n",* (This was during a period in my life when I refused to say "sir" to officers) *"that's the problem".*

Captain: *"You're going to be court marshaled, and you'll spend some serious time in the brig."*

Me: *"Good, I'll be happy to testify before a bunch of senior officers at my court marshal. I can point out when I repeatedly requested permission to shoot because we had 'hot guns' (against regulations), had open hatches all the way from the gun mount to the magazine (also against regulations) and had a round in the gun "cooking off", not one officer here in the chain of command had the presence of mind to do what was right and safe, and that was to fire the S. O. B. 's. The only alternative to me firing the guns was to sit here with my thumb up my ass, like everyone above me, and wait for the ship to blow up and kill half the crew."*

Everybody present, enlisted and officers alike, stood there with their mouths open and jaws on the floor.

The Captain, after about 10 seconds of pregnant silence, said, *"Well, don't let it happen again,"* and did an about face and beat feet out of there, followed by all his toadies. Not one word was ever spoken to me about it again. I seriously doubt that they even put it in the ships logs.

As an aside, this same Captain, (a few months later) while backing away from a pier in Mexico, backed the ship aground while taking depth soundings from the bow. Think about that. Taking depth readings from the bow while backing up. This act of incompetence wrecked   both our screws and shafts.

Very expensive! The Captain was not the only officer on the bridge, but no one dared stop him (assuming they even recognized how stupid he was). He kind of reminded me of a cross between 'Old Leadbottom' from the TV show 'McHale's Navy', and the Captain from 'The Caine Mutiny'.

3. We were having a torpedo drill / exercise and we lost the ability to charge the torpedo tube air flasks on the torpedo deck.

Now the air flasks that launch the torpedoes were under so much air pressure that if you jarred a charged flask while moving it, the pressure release could be akin to a grenade going off in your hands. Because of this you were to never transport charged flasks to--or from--the torpedo deck except under extreme emergency conditions (like war).

The command went down over the sound powered net that I was on (in Sonar Control) to the torpedo deck, to take the empty flask to engineering and charge it up, then carry the charged flask to the torpedo deck and proceed with the exercise. I immediately ordered the Torpedoman to not move till I got there. My Division Chief Petty Officer, three or four officers, and I converged on the torpedo deck at the same time. After explaining to the officers it was an unsafe and illegal order, and that we were not in an actual battle--but were only in a training exercise, the ASW Division Officer and Combat Officer both repeated the order to the Torpedoman. I then turned to the Torpedoman and, in front of them, said, *"They have just given you an unsafe and illegal order that you are under no obligation to follow. If you wish to follow their unsafe and illegal order it is totally up to you."* Dropped jaw time... The officers turned to the Chief, who shrugged his shoulders and said, "he's right". The Torpedo man very carefully did as they ordered, and nothing was ever said about it to me again.

I have many more sea stories, but this isn't my military memoir; there's no point in putting you to sleep.

The point of these anecdotes is to illustrate how incompetence and toadyism can be (at a minimum) dangerous, and even potentially fatal. If all officers had to go through a competency vetting process I would not have needed to step in and be insubordinate. It is worth noting because of these and other similar events I enjoyed a great deal of respect from the enlisted men (and even most officers) on the ship. To paraphrase an old TV commercial from a now-defunct brokerage house, "when I spoke, people listened". When I had a run-in with a new division officer (a brand new academy-puke who later gave me that less than sterling review), he went to our division Chief Petty Officer and insisted that I be written up for insubordination. The Chief responded, *"What did YOU do to piss Petty Officer Marxsen off?"* Upset by this response, he then went to his boss (Weapons Officer) to complain about both me, and what the Chief had said, and got a similar response, *"Well, what DID you do to piss him off?"* The result was--no write-up--just one really pissed off Ensign.

A number of years ago (1982, I believe) there was a book written that took the business world by storm, the title of which was **'In Search Of Excellence'** by Tom Peters. I remember thinking at the time, that without first being competent--the search for excellence is nothing but a Quixotic adventure that will (at best) have little chance in even attaining mediocrity. Thirty years later that book, its title, and my brother inspired me to write on this subject.

Because I feel the essence of competent leadership is founded in knowledge, here are some more quotes about knowledge I feel are appropriate to the difference between those who are competent, and those who are incompetent. I feel both those who wish to lead, as well as those who prefer to follow should heed these. These quotes are also relevant to the next three chapters on 'Strategic Thinking', 'Analytical Thinking', and 'Ethical Thinking'.

*There is one principle that can keep a man in everlasting ignorance. That is contempt prior to investigation...***Herbert Spencer.**

*The highest form of ignorance is when you reject something you don't know anything about...***Wayne Dyer.**

In short, a competent person has an open mind, will listen to evidence, and will choose a direction consistent with the facts and evidence (empirical--not anecdotal).

He who asks is a fool for five minutes, but he who does not ask remains a fool forever...**Chinese Proverb.**

Here's my all-time favorite for those who wish to be followers:

Men are four: He who knows not and knows not he knows not, he is a fool--shun him; He who knows not and knows he knows not, he is simple--teach him; He who knows and knows not he knows, he is asleep--wake him; He who knows and knows he knows, he is wise-- follow him...**Arabian proverb.**

The essence of knowledge is, having it--to apply it; not having it--to confess your ignorance...**Confucius**.

*The greatest obstacle to discovery is not ignorance - it is the **illusion** of knowledge*...**Daniel J Boorstin.**

The greatest of fools is he who imposes on himself, and in greatest concern, thinks certainly he knows that which he has studied, and of which he is profoundly ignorant--**Shaftsbury.**

The fundamental cause of trouble in the world is that the stupid are cocksure while the intelligent are full of doubt...**Bertrand Russell.**

*Suppose you were an Idiot, and suppose you were a member of Congress; but I repeat myself...***Mark Twain.** (That's a reflection of the intelligence of our elected leaders).

The final element to be added to competence (in my opinion) is consistency. The people you lead must not feel that you may / will change direction (or mind) often, or do so in an unpredictable manner--without good reason. You can, indeed, change your mind. However, it should be for a very good reason for those following to readily understand. Conversely, very few people want to follow a person that is intractable any more than they want to follow a person who changes constantly. I guess you could say a good leader has a need of being "flexibly firm".

It helps, and is even desirable, for a leader to be nice (and liked), but it is not absolutely necessary. Steve Jobs, Bill Gates, and Gen. George Patton were, by some accounts, not especially warm and fuzzy guys, but their overabundance of competence made up for that apparent shortfall.

Charismatic Leaders and Statutory Leaders enjoy temporary (albeit, sometimes longer than we prefer) success. They cannot hide their shortcomings forever, and are eventually removed from their leadership position. It can be quick and violent (as with revolution, assassination, or fragging), or quick and non-violent (as in elections, or firings), or gradual, such as when the followers gradually wise up and walk away shaking their heads at the stupidity of their leader.

The following is a reflection on the competence of some of our recent Commanders in Chiefs:

Sun Tzu: *When you engage in actual fighting, if victory is long in coming, then men's weapons will grow dull and their ardor will be damped. If you lay siege to a town, you will exhaust your strength. Again, if the campaign is protracted, the resources of the State will not be equal to the strain.*

Now, when your weapons are dulled, your ardor damped, your strength exhausted and your treasure spent, other chieftains will spring up to take advantage of your extremity. Then no man, however wise, will be able to avert the consequences that must ensue.

Thus, though we have heard of stupid haste in war, cleverness has never been seen associated with long delays.

There is no instance of a country having benefited from prolonged warfare.

It is only one who is thoroughly acquainted with the evils of war that can thoroughly understand the profitable way of carrying it on.

He will win who has military capacity and is not interfered with by the sovereign.

If some of our Presidents had read and understood Sun Tzu-- Korea, Viet Nam. Iraq and Afghanistan might have ended differently. Maybe they might have even--just--ended, or not have even started.

In case you hadn't figured it out on your own--these last Sun Tzu quotes are my thinly disguised jab at most of our Presidents after FDR; good examples of leaders who were, or are, incompetent--at least in regard to being our Commander in Chief (totally in charge of the military by law without regard to competence). They have been quick to say "Cry 'havoc' and let slip the dogs of war" (Julius Caesar... Shakespeare) quickly followed by their own "but keep them on a leash". If their own families and fortunes were at risk they might be a little more reticent to risk ours. After reading the chapter on "Strategic Thinking" you will see that they either had no strategy, or were extremely incompetent. I'm sorry, I just couldn't help myself. My disdain for most of our elected leaders keeps surfacing.

Leadership is competence (whose main ingredient is a large portion of knowledge) that is supported by Strategic Thinking, Analytical Thinking, and Ethical Thinking (the three legs of the three-legged leadership/competence seat). These are traits that all **"good"** leaders possess. This also is a slick segueing into this next chapter ('Strategic Thinking'), and the chapters after that ('Analytical Thinking' and 'Ethical Thinking').

Chapter 3

Strategic Thinking

In case you see the title of this chapter, and think, "that's for sales geeks", **Wait! Stop!** It's not just for sales geeks. Don't skip this chapter.

[My brother pointed out to me that there is already a mountain of books referencing Sun Tzu, and my sales anecdotes will bore people who aren't interested in sales. He suggested that I cut back on the sales anecdotes and add more of my military anecdotes (which he enjoys). There are two problems here. First my military experience allowed me to observe leadership but not strategy. That came later when I was in business and sales. Let me emphasize one thing--this is not a sales guide; everything that I will say--translates. The second problem is that while Sun Tzu has been the last arbiter of things strategic for 2500 years he has also been (and continues to be) the most ignored. Maybe this will be the catalyst that causes our leaders to start using their heads better. Please keep reading even if sales anecdotes bore you to tears.]

We **all** use (or **should** use) strategies every day. You use strategy in selling something, convincing your spouse you need a new car, wanting a promotion or raise, developing a business plan, or even campaigning for political office. Strategy is something we use without thinking very much about it. The problem is most of us have an approach we nearly always default to; and that strategy is more often than not far from the best. Also, many people who profess to understand strategies really don't; they most likely have remembered a few sound bites from Sun Tzu's 'The Art Of War'. For example, most people (when on the subject of Sun Tzu) give a wise nod and say "Keep your friends close, but keep your enemies closer". That quote didn't come from Sun Tzu. In fact, it cannot be found in written form (anywhere) prior to the movie/book 'Godfather II', written by Mario Puzo. 99 % of all the people whom I have met, who said that they read Sun Tzu's 'The Art of War', were blowing smoke. They didn't have the patience to really read it (there are no Cliff's Notes available). What does that do to the credibility of all those people who have repeated that supposed quote? I have read 'The Art of War', and it was extraordinarily tedious and boring. It is a translation accompanied by an interpretation (and sometimes multiple and conflicting interpretations) after every stanza. Imagine 'The Bible' loaded with so many notes, footnotes, and academic opinions, that it overwhelms the text. It wasn't until I took a digital copy and stripped out all the extraneous b. s. that I was then able to get through it without becoming cross-eyed and falling asleep.

I had the privilege of attending some 'Strategic Selling' and 'Power Based Selling' seminars, both of which were conducted by Jim Holden (of The Holden Corp) about 30 years ago while I was at Schlumberger.

My apologies to Mr. Holden for anything which I may forget here, but the basics in strategic thinking are as follows:

[Note: I have no connection with Holden, and indeed, haven't even had contact with them since attending their seminars 30 years ago. But assuming they are still in business I recommend everyone in management, marketing, and sales, attend one or more of their courses.]

A strategy is the **overall** plan and approach for achieving a defined goal, as well as the plan for the distribution and positioning of resources. Strategies and Tactics are essentially both the same thing, except Tactics are subordinate to Strategies, and are used to serve the Strategy. Tactics can be altered as necessary to adjust to changing conditions. Strategies, once settled on, should, if possible, not be changed. That bears repeating. **A strategy, when designed properly, should never be changed except in extraordinary circumstances.**

47

When most people talk about strategies--what they are really referring to is tactics, and don't know the difference.

[Note: While I use sales situations, sports, and the military as examples because they are the easiest to understand and visualize, just translate them to other situations (they are, after all, similes); it works the same--regardless.]

The eight steps involved in designing a strategy are as follows:

These first four steps are what we'll call **"Get The Big Picture"**.

You'll notice the simplistic drawings I am including as illustrations are truly worth a thousand words. I didn't come up with them (I remembered them from Jim Holden).

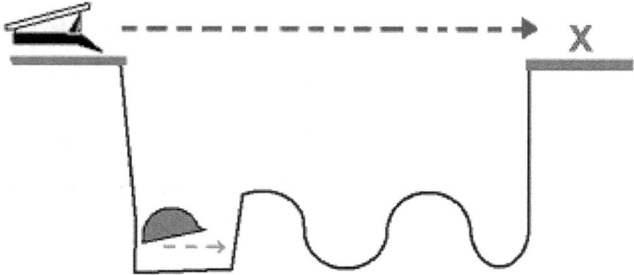

Here is an anecdote that well illustrates the benefit of getting the big picture.

When I was a Sonar Technician-Second Class (Second Class Petty Officer) on my Destroyer and we were getting out of dry dock (in-between my two trips to Viet Nam), the Sonar gang, Combat, and Bridge crew (with all the appropriate officers) traveled to San Diego to the Fleet Anti-Submarine Warfare Training Center (FASWTC) to go through the ASW simulators in order to freshen up our ASW (Anti-Submarine Warfare) skills. Since I had Sonar and ASROC down pat, the decision was made to see if I could handle the ASW officers' job, just in case back up was ever needed. During our time on the simulators I sufficiently impressed the instructors, who in turn, influenced our officers enough to decide I was to act as the ASW officer the following week when our ship would be on the test range for live exercises against a submerged target.

During a live practice, observers often inserted problems and strange events into the exercise, just as they do in the simulator to evaluate how everyone reacts.

Anyway during this practice, Sonar reported contact, and as the acting ASW officer I was given the Con of the ship, as well as control of the ASW weapons. This is done because the ASW officer is supposed to have the most complete understanding of what is happening, and how to best prosecute an attack.

Here, my brother suggested I might want to include a small note for the non-navy people what port, starboard, bow, aft, stern, etc. means so they do not get lost in this story. So for you land lubbers. Bow is front, stern, aft and abaft is back, starboard is right, port is left, and abeam is to the side.

I directed the bridge to make the ship come left 20 degrees to turn the ship so the submerged target would then line up about 800 yards off our port bow, moving aft; and at the same time, I said, *"Torpedo, Sonar, train port tubes 45 degrees to port, prep torpedo tube one, 0 degrees gyro."*

Torpedo deck: *"Ready".*

Me: *"Torpedo, Sonar, Shoot".* This all happened within the first ten to fifteen seconds of gaining contact. The official protocol at the time (again, if I remember right) was that you needed to get a weapon in the water within 30 seconds, so the submarine would have to perform evasive maneuvers (and as a result) ruin its fire control solution. It doesn't even have to be aimed in the right direction; just shoot something (anything) in any direction, and it will force them to perform evasive maneuvers.

Torpedo deck: *"Sonar, Torpedo, Port tube malfunctioning".* By this time, the target was off our port beam, sliding aft.

Me: *"Torpedo, Sonar, Prep starboard tubes (so far-so good) starboard 140 degrees, prep torpedo tube one, set gyro right 70 degrees".* (What?)

Torpedo deck: *"Sonar, Torpedo, ready".*

Me: *"Torpedo, Sonar, shoot".*

The torpedo shot out on the starboard side towards the stern, sank 30 feet, spun up, turned right 70 degrees, crossed under and behind the stern of the ship, went straight toward the target, and got a hit.

The observers in Sonar asked, *"What in the world was that?"* (Well, actually the language was more colorful than that.)

I told them:

1. The torpedo tubes could safely be trained aft and fired.

2. The torpedoes are disabled above a 30-foot depth, so it could safely cross under our stern if we haven't gotten clear.

3. Setting in that specific gyro preset tells the torpedo to run on a search course after making an initial turn of 70 degrees to the right.

The result was to put the torpedo on a direct course for the target even though it was on the opposite side of the ship--going away.

Their response was *"But that's not protocol".*

I said the protocol dictates a weapon in the water within 30 seconds, period. That shot took less than 30 seconds. Also, it is incredibly stupid to waste an expensive torpedo with a miss, still leaving the ship in danger, when (with a little competence) you can kill the target with the same effort and time. It was, indeed, according to protocol--unless, of course, I was supposed to have **intentionally** missed the enemy. I then said, **"All you have to do is have the big picture and know the capabilities of your weapons systems."**

They went away shaking their heads and mumbling.

The following week, when we all were at FASWTC for a formal critique, we were told that was the most creative shot (backwards, behind the back and cross-under) they had yet seen. But while they were really impressed, the existing protocol and training stands; they were not going to try to teach anyone else how to do it. Their reasoning was they didn't think many others could duplicate it, as well as the indecision and resulting errors could be fatal to those ships and crews attempting it.

When we got back to the ship, the new Captain reassigned our ASW Officer to other duties, and assigned me as the acting ASW Officer during general quarters (battle stations) for submarine action, also called condition 1AS.

How important is getting the big picture? There's the old story that comes to mind of the three blind men who were introduced to an elephant and   asked to describe the animal.

The first blind man feels only the trunk and thereafter confidently describes the beast as a great snake-like creature, similar to a python. The second blind man feels only the elephant's ears and announces that it is a bird that can soar to great heights. The third blind man examines only the fringe-tipped fly-chasing tail and "sees" an animal that is curiously like a bottlebrush. In other words, if you don't get the big picture-it is very easy to be not only wrong, but also not even have the right genus.

Sun Tzu*: If you know the enemy and know yourself, you need not fear the result of a hundred battles. If you know yourself but not the enemy, for every victory gained you will also suffer a defeat. If you know neither the enemy nor yourself, you will succumb in every battle.*

Honest to god, I never heard of Sun Tzu until at least ten years later. And by the way, that quote is as close as Sun Tzu comes to *"keep your friends close, but keep your enemies closer"*.

Hey, I'm getting pretty good at this segueing stuff. Check this next section out.

Step 1. Understand Your Enemy (Objective)

This is the first thing that must be done when developing a strategy. It can be as formal, complex and time consuming as

53

you want, or as quick and simple as the situation calls for. In the case of one-call sales calls, which can be in person or even on the phone, the process is greatly accelerated and limiting. The more abbreviated or truncated the process--the less the likelihood of success. Hence the lower success rates of one visit sales cold calls and telemarketing. In the case of big-ticket sales, it takes much more time and resources to develop the proper amount of intelligence needed to devise a proper strategy because of what is at stake. In any case, the more you understand about the opposition--the better are your chances of success.

I used to start every potential sale with a multi-page form that was provided by Holden. This form not only formalized all these steps, but also became an account record, profile, and progress report. This report could be quickly read by me or anyone else from the company whom I needed to quickly understand what the situation or status was.

The first thing you came to in this form was a large empty rectangle at the top of the inside cover page. The purpose of this space was to draw an organization chart of the management and key players within the customer's organization. Each customer's name and title was represented in an individual box and with lines of authority connecting the individual boxes (basically, an organization chart). Additionally, drawing a line encircling them identified the influential groups or cliques. Lastly, since every group or clique has a person who influences that group, an X is placed in that person's box identifying him or her as the fox, or "Le Renard" (as Jim Holden called them). This influential person may or may not be the boss or head of the group, but is the person when a point is made (in a meeting or presentation), everyone looks at to gauge his or her reaction. This "fox" designation is also topic specific. When I was a technician at GTE (even before I was promoted to management) I was "Le Renard" with regard to technical issues, in spite of the fact that there were degreed engineers in those groups and meetings.

In the case of dealing with multiple business units or locations, each business unit or location got their own supplemental chart, with the main chart on the first page becoming an overall chart at the corporate and business unit level.

Step 2. Understand the terrain (physical and political environment)

Then to this form notations were made to indicate the attitudes, positions, concerns, plans and goals each player had. Also it was used to indicate alliances and influences that could affect a successful outcome for me.

If this just seems unnecessary or way too complicated, it isn't.

What you get out of your strategy is directly related to what you put into it. Or, as we used to say in regard to problems with computer programs, 'Garbage In--Garbage Out'. The higher the stakes--the more effort needed to ensure success.

The less politics, agendas, or resources influence a strategy-- the greater the chances of having a successful strategy. To put it another way--politics, agendas and resources are the limiting factors when determining strategies. With a risk of being redundant, a perfect (and realistic) strategy can always be determined as long as it does not have to also satisfy any needs and desires (politics, agendas, and resources) external to the desired goal. One need look no further than **all** the wars and conflicts the United States has been involved in (starting with the Korean War), to see how politics has screwed up any possibility of succeeding in those same conflicts. Of course, I am presuming winning those conflicts was the goal. If winning wasn't the goal then maybe the strategies were actually successful, though, with extraordinary costs in both lives and treasure.

Sun Tzu: *One may KNOW how to conquer without being able to DO it.*

Some extreme and hypothetical examples that support that quote are: 1) The Baptist Church would NEVER agree to elect anyone from Islam to manage their church (of course, that is an assumption), even if it were in their best interest to do so; (2) A wife who is adamantly against polygamy will NOT be persuaded to allow her husband to bring another woman into their marriage, unless, of course, the two of them have twelve kids and she needs the help (if that is your situation, go for it); (3) Your boss will not tolerate a strategy which shows him to have been stupid, or in error (even if he is both). As the following anecdote illustrates, I have "been there, and done that".

When I was working for a publishing company, as National Sales Manager, we had a problem with 'DEXPO', one of our trade shows. This semi-annual trade show was a show that the company had purchased a year or two earlier for over twenty million dollars, and was bringing in a few million dollars annually in profit. The show was held every autumn in the West and every spring in the East, in conjunction with the 'DECUS' (Digital Equipment Corporation Users Symposium) conventions. It was a prime place for sellers of computer equipment and software products to make contacts with (and sell their products to) users, and potential users, of DEC computers as well as other computer vendors.

The problem arose when the 'DECUS' users group, realizing the amount of resulting profits from the show, decided to own and produce their own trade show in order for their "not for profit" association to better fund its needs and desires. As a result the exhibitors were torn between wanting to be part of our production, while leaning toward exhibiting with the new show because the **owners** of that show were also the very **customers** that they were seeking.

In a management meeting to determine what to do, I first asked, *"This is a trade show that relies on an outside association for its attendees; didn't we get any contractual obligations from the association before we purchased the show?"* Everyone looked at me like I was a Martian speaking Swahili.

I then asked. *"Has anyone pointed out to 'DECUS' how much is involved in actually producing a trade show?"* The answer was, *"yes; they are contracting another trade show company to produce it for them."*

I then asked if we had approached DECUS to make them a "Strategic Partner"? The answer was, *"yes; we offered them about three hundred thousand a year to drop it and stick with our show."*

I said, *"That is only around 10% of the profit generated; why would they accept that--when they can have the whole enchilada? I'm talking about a joint ownership--real partners".*

From the expressions on their faces you'd think that I had just passed some really bad gas. As the Bible (Old Testament) frequently says, *"there was much wailing, and gnashing of teeth"*. They had paid over twenty million dollars for that show, and were not about to GIVE part of it away. And certainly they were not going to cede any amount of control over to them. No! NEVER! The answer had to be in improved production values, or strengthening vendor alliances. I then said that the problem is the vendors would go where their customers were, and their customers owned that show. And, there was nothing we could do to change that. If we wanted to keep sole ownership of the show (and survive), then we would have to move it to different areas of the country and different times of the year; and give money to (and work with) the 'DECUS' Regional Chapters, instead of the National Association. The "new" show would survive, albeit at a greatly reduced profitability. The response was, "No, we paid too much money for a national show to then regionalize it and make much less money". Again, the answer **just had to be** improved production values and vendor alliances.

There wasn't a strategic thinker among them.

We then pulled out all the stops (and check book) in order to improve production values; and wined and dined our exhibitors, and then still held our show at the same time, and in the same city, as our new rival (which was owned by our target audience).

It (predictably) didn't work. The political constraint hamstrung us. The boss (who paid too much and negotiated a bad contract) wanted us to save him without having to expose him. He was fired within a year of my departure.

I ran into the following flaw a lot in this company. They would always proceed under the assumption their product was the show, and had no idea what I was talking about when I would say, *"No, our product is the delivering of quality show-attendee's to our exhibitors (who are our customers as well as our clients). The show is just the tool we use for attracting those attendees."*

They not only didn't know their product, they didn't know our customers (exhibitors), or our customers-customer (attendees), but they also put unrealistic political constraints on any potential strategy.

They probably would have done very well in the political arena.

Hence the previous Sun Tzu quote; *"One may KNOW how to conquer without being able to DO it."* **And another (related);** *"He will win who has military capacity and is not interfered with by the sovereign."*

Step- 3. Understand what your resources are.

The third step in the process was to list all the resources at your disposal.

These were not only things like demo equipment I had access to, but also included people such as Product Managers, Application Engineers, and Senior Management. It also included access to facilities and meeting rooms--essentially anything that could be utilized to aid the strategy.

One resource sales people like to use is customer testimonials. I took it a step further. When I was a Sales Engineer and later a Sales Manager at Schlumberger, one of the products I sold was a piece of automatic test equipment used to diagnose and repair the electronic circuit boards of machines and robots used in other company's manufacturing processes. These "boxes" cost between one hundred to one hundred fifty thousand dollars each, so it would require a full court press due to the customers needing to get it into the next year's budget. As such, the sales usually took about a year or more to accomplish.

I used to arrange for my customers to give demonstrations on their equipment--in their facilities--to other companies. Within the heavy equipment manufacturing community I used Cadillac to meet with and demo to customers who were not only from other GM divisions, but also customers from John

Deere, International, and Caterpillar, etc. I would also use the non-automobile manufacturing customer-users to meet with and demo at their facilities, to Ford and Chrysler. Not only did these people give a better demo (with greater credibility) than we could, but most of the time my customer-demonstrators would ask for the order and close the sale for me. I'm not kidding; Strategic thinking really does make everything easier.

When you make an exhaustive and detailed list of your resources, you will be better able to see your strengths as well as your weaknesses. As an example; even though a football coach might wish to implement a 'west coast offense' the coach wouldn't be able to implement it if the quarterback has a low pass-completion percentage or has receivers who cannot hold onto a football once it got there.

Step 4. Identify the goal and keep it simple (Strategic Statement)

This can be the hardest thing to accomplish in designing a good strategy.

The strategic statement should be short and concise. MacArthur's strategy to win back the Pacific was to "Island hop". Eisenhower's strategy to beat the Germans in Europe was to make the Germans fight a two front war to divide their forces and conquer them more easily. Neither General was concerned with public opinion or politics with regard to their strategies

When you consider the strategies used in all our wars since WWII, none of them were clear and concise. The inclusion of political considerations and desires muddied them all. The goal in Korea and Viet Nam was not necessarily to win, but to "stop the Commies." Our strategies in Afghanistan and Iraq were muddied by the need to have good PR, and to negotiate with anyone and everyone. The lack of success in Afghanistan and Iraq is also because of the military's mandate to defeat the enemy (whoever that was), while at the same time not causing too much collateral damage or civilian casualties. As a result, we have faced a bunch of forever-wars. The exception was Viet Nam, which, by the way, we pulled out of because we refused to try to win. Afghanistan and Iraq will have the same result. The fault of these strategic failures does not lie with the Generals, but with our political leadership who wouldn't know a proper strategy if you hit them over the head with one.

Hint--a good strategy does not include the word **"but"**, as in, "defeat the enemy, **but** don't hurt anyone. A politician's talent and goal is to talk and spin, and get what they want (politically) so they can get re-elected.

Hence this quote by **Sun Tzu:** *He will win who has military capacity and is* *not interfered with by the sovereign.*

K.I.S.S. (Keep It Simple, Stupid; not the rock group) is a concept applicable to the successful design of anything and everything, regardless whether it is a widget, fashion, or strategy.

Step-5. Identify the strategy

Now we get to the part that everyone has been (or should have been) waiting for, the strategies.

There are just five basic strategies, and every strategy you conceive or encounter will be a variation or permutation of one of them.

The Basic Five Strategies:

DIRECT $\longrightarrow \longleftarrow \mathsf{X}$

The Direct strategy is the one that is most often used, and (unfortunately) is the one, which is easiest to defeat. It is the default strategy of choice by most people, mostly because it requires no thought or understanding.

A direct strategy is basically a head-to-head--my strength against your strength, approach. In football it is an offensive running game between the tackles into an "eight in the box" defense.

The old fashioned duel was a direct strategy.

A couple of good examples of failed direct strategies are:

The French Maginot Line at the beginning of WWII. (The French didn't read Sun Tzu.). The Germans went around it and over it.

Egypt, turning their tank force into a modern version of the Maginot Line against the quick and nimble (read mobile) Israeli tank force (1967, or 1973, I don't remember--one of their ongoing reruns). They must not have read Sun Tzu, or learned the lessons of the failed French strategy.

Saddam Hussein's insistence on turning his tank corps into a modern version of the Maginot Line (during the Gulf War). No Kidding! Not only did he ignore Sun Tzu, but he also ignored the fact that the Maginot Line was a failure, as well as the same spectacular failure by the Egyptians using this **same strategy** about seventeen years earlier.

George Santayana--*Those who cannot remember the past are condemned to repeat it.*

The problem is when playing only to your strengths; your strengths may not be good enough or match up properly with your opponents' weaknesses. And, when it's not good enough--what then? For a Direct Strategy to succeed your opponent must not only be weaker, but must also be unimaginative. Hence the very predictable failures of France, Egypt, and Iraq.

The trade-show example previously cited (an example of how one may know in theory how to conquer, without being able to pull it off) is a perfect example of a "Direct Strategy" that didn't work.

Sun Tzu--_In all fighting, the direct method may be used for joining battle, but indirect methods will be needed in order to secure victory._

[Nice of Mr. Tzu to provide for me a perfect segue into my next strategy.]

INDIRECT

Sun Tzu--_Indirect tactics, efficiently applied, are inexhaustible as Heaven and Earth, unending as the flow of rivers and streams; like the sun and moon, they end but to begin anew; like the four seasons, they pass away to return_ *once more.*

In order to make this rather nebulous quote more easily understood: You use an indirect strategy to simply change the ground rules to those that favor you. The possibilities for indirect strategies are as endless as your imagination.

In football, the forward pass, play action pass, option and flanker reverse, are all indirect strategies.

During the American Revolution, the introduction of Guerrilla Warfare was a game changing Indirect Strategy.

At the beginning of WWII the Germans, instead of attacking the Maginot Line, which was the strength of the French defense, simply went over, and around it. Yuup, indirect.

In the Gulf War, instead of attacking Hussein's superior tank-force of thousands of dug-in tanks head-on, the U.S. went over, and around them… Duh!!!

MacArthur's Island hopping was an Indirect Strategy.

Boxing legend Ali's "rope-a-dope" was an Indirect Strategy. He couldn't see any benefit in going toe-to-toe trading punches with a monster slugger like George Foreman.

In basketball, the four-corners offense is an Indirect Strategy. If your opponents' strength is speed, and you cannot keep up with them, then slow the game down to make it a game of efficiency and accuracy.

You may recall in my aforementioned trade-show debacle, the strategies I had suggested were to either make the users group our partners, or distance ourselves from them entirely (both physically, and time-wise). Both were indirect strategies. Because we went with a direct strategy, the end result was the complete writing off of a twenty million dollar investment.

"Spin" is also an indirect strategy. The object of "spin" is to get your target to focus on (or believe in) something else in order to get the result that you want. In the King James Version (translation/interpretation) of the Bible there is a reference to "men stealers" as opposed to the accurate translation of "slave traders". This was allegedly done to appease the nobility of the time who made a great deal of money in the slave trade. Also, the Bible translations prior to the King James Version were less sympathetic to the rule of royalty; so it makes sense that the version authorized and sponsored by King James would correct that "mistake".

In other words "Spin", as an Indirect Strategy, is changing the ground rules when the current rules don't favor you. "Spin" can be honest, or it can be dishonest; its ethics, or morality, lies entirely with the person who is doing the "spinning".

Uh, is it clear to you by now that I really--**really**--do not like "spin", or those who choose   to be "spinners? When you couple the desire of someone to "spin" with a person who is a lawyer (who by vocation and training adopt a standard of ethics that ignores right from wrong), you will understand why I consider most politicians to be (to borrow a term used in Navy Boot Camp--when referring to new recruits) "lower than whale shit". That is pretty low when you consider how deep the ocean is, and you've never seen it floating.

While I was V.P. of Sales at a competitor to Schlumberger I was selling an automatic tester that was a direct competitor to the unit that I had sold for Schlumberger. This unit, while more than adequate for the job, was not as technically slick as the one from Schlumberger. The one feature ours had (and Schlumberger's did not) was the ability to generate schematics as a by-product of programming the machine. One of the customers to whom I was selling was a company that repaired circuit boards (for anybody, and on anything), and they usually could not get schematics for their own use. I emphasized to them while our tester would do a more than adequate job of diagnosing and fixing bad circuit boards, it would also solve their need to reverse engineer many of the circuit boards they received for repair. Reverse engineering not only helps in understanding the circuit board, but it also makes programming the tester easier and faster. That was an indirect strategy (and spin). Change the way the customer perceives his needs.

Most, but not all, successful strategies are indirect.

DIVIDE AND
CONQUER

Sun Tzu--_We can form a single united body, while the enemy must split up into fractions. Hence there will be a whole pitted against separate parts of a whole, which means that we shall be many to the enemy's few. And if we are able thus to attack an inferior force with a superior one, our opponents will be in dire straits._

The prosecution of WWII in Europe was a perfect example of Divide and Conquer. In spite of Stalin's constant plea's and insistence the Allies join the Soviet Union on the eastern front to help him fight Germany, the Allies held fast to their conviction the best way to defeat Germany was to make Germany fight a war on two fronts, thus dividing their forces and making each front weaker and more vulnerable to defeat.

In football the screen pass is a Divide and Conquer strategy.

The problem with the Divide and Conquer strategy is there is a perfect counter-strategy that can often work well against it.

When you think about the above quote from Sun Tzu, you can't help but understand that since a divided force is more easily defeated, then it must be paramount not to have your own forces divided. Hitler never understood this, and neither apparently did George Custer.

General George Custer, in the last couple of weeks of the Civil War, got a stunning victory over the Confederates by dividing his unit into three smaller units and attacking the numerically superior enemy from three different directions. This was not a sound strategy, but worked because his enemy was in retreat, starving, and low on supplies.

Later, at the Little Big Horn, he applied this same bold strategy. That is, divide his forces into three disconnected units and attack the Sioux from three different directions. The Sioux were not in retreat, not starving nor low on supplies In fact, the Sioux were itching for a fight. Custer (and his unfortunate men) then paid the price for his being stupid (notice, I didn't say he wasn't brave). In Custer's defense, there were no good translations (at the time) of Sun Tzu's 'The Art of War'. Read this quote below.

Sun Tzu--*Do not repeat the tactics that have gained you one victory, but let your methods be regulated by the infinite variety of circumstances.*

If you look at the above illustration for the Divide and Conquer Strategy, you may notice that it would be relatively easy for those divided forces to turn inward, and meet up, cutting off the dividing force from the rear; resulting in a "Surround and Harass", or Siege. (See below.)

Man, talk about a slick segueing into the next strategy. This book writing stuff is easy-peezy.

Sun Tzu-- *Thus the highest form of generalship is to balk the enemy's plans; the next best is to prevent the junction of the enemy's forces; the next in order is to attack the enemy's army in the field; and the worst policy of all is to besiege walled cities.*

Surround and Harass is basically a siege strategy. You surround your opponent and deny them movement (or support) in (or from) any direction. In other words, you isolate your opponent.

In football, flooding a zone with receivers is a Surround and Harass strategy.

The siege of Masada in ancient Israel was a "Surround and Harass" strategy used by the Romans. In fact, in ancient times the Siege strategy was used quite often. It is used much less today because, as Sun Tzu indicates, it is the weakest of all strategies. It can, however, make a good counter-strategy when used at the tactic level, as you will see in my next anecdote.

I was working as a Sales Manager at a company that produced automated IC (integrated circuits) handlers, automated IC testers, and automated "pick and place" circuit board assemblers in the mid 1980's when I started to develop Delco as a customer for our IC testers. Delco (Kokomo, IN) was a big customer of our IC handlers, but they only used old Schlumberger testers for their small and medium scale IC's. They were going to upgrade to large scale and very large scale IC's in a year or so. They would need from seventy to one hundred forty testers (depending on configuration) selling at a price of seven hundred fifty thousand dollars to one and a half million dollars each (again, depending on configuration). As you will see why later, Schlumberger was not going to be considered for future purchases. GenRad had sold a few testers there and had established a beachhead.

Kokomo did not want to go out on a limb and be the first (in Delco) to try another new tester. So my strategy was going to be "Divide and Conquer". I needed to successfully get a tester into another Delco division and parlay that into success in Kokomo. No problem.

Delco had another division in Milwaukee, WI, with which I also had a long and good relationship with, who also was thinking about getting an automatic IC tester for receiving inspections. The problem there was the engineering department, although they had good connections and rapport with Kokomo, had a direct connection with Delco in Thousand Oaks, CA.

Thousand Oaks had just bought a GenRad tester. Apparently GenRad had the same strategy as me. Divide and Conquer.

I then, started to work on Thousand Oaks (because they were the influencing factor) with help and advice from Milwaukee. I soon discovered the Lead Engineer who made the buying decision (the person, 'Le Renard', through whom I had to go) was very emotionally invested in GenRad and was not going to budge. He had made the buying decision, and even though our alternative tester didn't exist when he was going through the evaluation process, he didn't want to look like he made a wrong decision. He was also an empire builder who was proud of the amount of money he was authorized to spend (our tester cost almost half of what the GenRad did). I was going to have to use a counter strategy of Surround and Harass as a local tactic to neutralize his influence in order to succeed at a higher level. In other words, I was going to have to neutralize him by isolating and pressuring him with every one around him, including his bosses.

This engineer (who had a very petulant personality) was reluctant to allow me to come to Thousand Oaks and give a presentation to him and his upper management. So my contacts in Milwaukee used their managers to convince his managers to invite me there to give them a presentation.

At the very start of the presentation, in a glass enclosed conference room, this engineer stated, *"I don't know why you bothered to come here; I'm not interested in anything you have to say!"* He then picked up his chair, turned it around 180 degrees, and sat down again with his back to me--in front of God, his bosses and co-workers. You could have heard a pin drop in that room. He had just committed political suicide within Delco by doing this in front of his bosses. I had hoped I could get him to do or say something stupid, but this was far beyond anything that I had hoped for; and I hadn't said a word yet. After an appropriate short silence on my part, I commenced with my presentation as if nothing had happened. At the end of the meeting the Lead Engineers' superiors came up to me and apologized for his being so rude, thanked me for the presentation, and said they had heard of nothing but good things about me (and my company) from both Milwaukee and Kokomo. That Bozo had placed himself in a siege, with no help from me.

When I got back to Chicago (home) my contacts in Milwaukee called me to tell me the Thousand Oaks upper management had contacted their management team and told them if my tester is what they wanted, go for it.

Like the immortal, strategic genius, **Hannibal Smith** (a character in the TV-show 'The A-Team') was wont to say, *"I love it when a plan comes together"*.

The GenRad sales team was not thinking strategically; or at the very least they took their eye off the ball while thinking they had everything under control. They should have coached the Delco engineer on how to respond and control the meeting.

In WWII, Hitler initiated the 'Battle of the Bulge' in an effort to divide and conquer, but his attacking forces ended up being surrounded, and lost.

The recommendation resulting from these examples and the Custer debacle is to be very alert and careful when trying a Divide and Conquer strategy because it can too easily be turned into a Surround and Harass counter strategy against you.

SCORCHED EARTH

The fifth and last strategy (Scorched Earth) works, but should be used rarely (if at all).

The purpose of Scorched Earth is to deny your enemy by destroying anything and everything of the enemy's that can be used (to advantage) against you.

A classic example of Scorched Earth is Sherman's March to the sea in the Civil War. His army systematically burned and destroyed everything in a wide swath from Atlanta, GA to Savannah, GA, denying food, shelter, and supplies, not only to the Confederate army, but also to the civilian population who supported them.

Stalin also did (to his own Russia) the same thing during the Soviet retreat in the face of the German advance. This denied the Germans food and shelter and, with the oncoming winter, cost the Germans dearly.

The strategic bombing campaign in WWII was also an example of Scorched Earth; obliterating centers of industry that supported the German war effort.

Dropping nuclear weapons on Japan was an obvious extreme example of "Scorched Earth".

In the Old Testament of The Bible, God was constantly telling the Israelites to destroy everyone and everything; all men, women and children, cities, animals, and crops, and to leave nothing standing when engaging the countries they were supposed to conquer. And according to the bible God punished those Israelites who showed mercy… Scorched Earth…

Some immature people (mostly children), when faced with losing a game, will take the ball and go home, or tip the game board over, thus denying their opponents the enjoyment of finishing the game. Saddam Hussein set fire to the oil wells in Iraq, rather than letting them fall into our hands. Those are good examples of Scorched Earth.

In my introduction I mentioned I left Schlumberger at odds over their desire to use such a strategy with a customer. I was losing in the possible sale of one of Schlumberger's testers to a tester from Everett/Charles. Everett Charles was a previous employer, and both of those testers I had significant input on the design. Everett/Charles execution of my concept was better than Schlumberger's. The customer was Delco (Milwaukee).

My management wanted me to set up a strategy to do to the key people at Milwaukee in the same manner I (a couple of years later) would do to set up the Lead Engineer from Thousand Oaks to do to himself; which was to destroy them. I didn't want to do so, as I had a very good relationship with those people and their management. I felt that if I screwed them I would destroy any chance of my selling anything to that company (or those people) in the future.

My bosses (the National Sales Manager, and the Business Unit Manager) insisted I set up a   meeting with the key people and management of Delco (Milwaukee), The strategy was to be a last ditch effort so we could save the sale. And, if we couldn't save the sale we would "poison the well" so Everett/Charles wouldn't get the business either.

Reluctantly, after considerable argument (and wailing and gnashing of teeth) I set the meeting up. In the car on the way to the customer meeting, my boss told me to make the introductions, keep quiet, and to *"let me show how it's done"*. When my contact met us in Delco's lobby, he gave me an odd look, and said to my boss (rather coolly), *"I don't know what the purpose of this meeting is, but welcome, and follow me."*

At the start of the meeting I made the introductions, and, as instructed, turned the meeting over to my boss, who then said (the coward), *"Larry has something he wanted to say!"*

After taking a few seconds thinking up something to say, I then gave a last ditch pitch to save the sale without screwing anyone. It didn't work.

On our way out, my contact pulled me aside, and said, *"I know what they were trying to do. I want you to know you are welcome here anytime. And in the future I will be happy to purchase from you anything that is not from Schlumberger. Also--in the future, Schlumberger will not sell anything to me, to my people, or anywhere in Delco, or anywhere that I, or my people might go (should we leave Delco)."* And that (dear friends) is exactly what happened. Schlumberger did not renew my contract because my bosses were uncomfortable having a witness to their screw-up. Instead, I started my Sales Rep. Company with them (Schlumberger) as my first vendor. Incidentally, they never--**ever**--allowed start-ups to sell their products, except for me.

Schlumberger never sold another piece of equipment to Delco, and I eventually sold a whole lot of other very expensive equipment into Delco and General Motors. I just did it for someone else.

Schlumbergers' automated test equipment business units eventually ceased operations in North America because of attitudes like this, and an overall lack of understanding of the automated test equipment market. They got into the automated test equipment market by purchasing each of the leading companies in each market category, and then within ten years their market share shrank to near zero in each of those same market niches. They tried to run our U. S. high tech companies with the successful business models from their oil field services, and which they also used successfully in Europe.

I am now going to beat you over the head with the moral of that story.

The problem with "poisoning the well" (as it were) is after doing so you cannot yourself drink from the same well. You've made the decision to ruin it for everyone who drinks not only from that well, but also from all wells in the future, which are connected to it. It is not usually a viable long-term strategy.

Scorched Earth is a very useful strategy when used in war. But, due to the dire consequences, I consider the Scorched Earth strategy to be a non-option outside of war. Use it only at your peril. Outside of war, the only people who use Scorched Earth are petulant, self-absorbed, and who are doomed to long-term failure.

Here is a dead horse that deserves another beating: **Whenever possible; use an Indirect Strategy.**

Step- 6. Determine the tactics and timeline.

The next steps in the strategic process, based on the form, were to determine the tactics to be used, the needed resources, and then assign everything to a formal timeline. This timeline could be a graph-like illustration, or a numbered outline (whichever you favor), but it is very important to formalize this process because forgetting is not an option.

Step- 7. Test the strategy (without bias).

The seventh step in developing your strategy is to test it. This is harder than it appears. You must be absolutely unbiased and not married to your choice of strategies. Try to develop an honest counter-strategy from your opponents' perspective in order to test for weaknesses. This means you will have to do an honest and thorough analysis of your opponents' capabilities, resources, and politics. If you find you have trouble doing this, get someone else whom you trust to test it. Writers need editors for the same reason; they are too close to their product to be objective. You should have seen this book before someone else edited it.

Step- 8. Assign the resources necessary to reach your goal.

The eighth, and final step, is self-evident; assign the resources (according to the timeline) necessary for reaching your goal (the Order of Battle--if you will).

The neat side- benefit that resulted from this formal process (and the form) that I used became evident when I would be driving a manager, salesman, applications engineer, or even a strategic partner to an account I would hand the form to them so they could acquaint themselves with (and be briefed on) the situation and what was necessary to be accomplished. We would then very literally be on the same page. After finishing reading the form, the look on their faces was priceless... Definitely NOT your average sales geek!

Utilizing this process of thinking strategically can have benefits that go beyond winning more often. It makes you more analytical in your overall thinking. And, aside from gaining more respect from your customer, it opens up more opportunities. I had an Independent Sales Rep who worked for me, and he liked to have me go with him on sales calls-- especially if there was going to be a plant tour. Most sales people have blinders on, and are so focused on their products and prospects, when inundated by the kind of information to be gleaned from a plant tour they don't connect the dots (how's that for a mixed metaphor). By paying close attention and asking questions about their processes I was able to predict what their needs were going to be, regardless whether it would involve us or not. My Sales Rep would then go out and get a contract with a vendor who could meet those eventual needs, resulting in more sales orders for him and his company.

If you utilize this kind of strategic thinking for any length of time it becomes second nature to the way you view and approach nearly everything. You will be able to see through the B.S. that we are all constantly bombarded with on a daily basis. It is the epitome of the P5R rule, which is: Prior Planning Prevents Piss-Poor Results (I'm sorry, I didn't come up with that on my own; I lifted it from a Stephen Coonts novel). Even investing in the stock market will become easier and much more profitable.

To sum it all up, 'Strategic Thinking' contributes to your competence and credibility. All that is left to make you a supremely competent leader is the ability to "Design", and "Do Right".

Chapter 4

Analytical Thinking

Sherlock Holmes (A Study in Scarlet, by Sir Arthur Conan Doyle): *In solving a problem of this sort the grand thing is to be able to reason backwards. That is a very useful accomplishment and a very real one, but people do not practice it much. In the every day affairs of life it is more useful to reason forwards, and so the other becomes neglected. There are fifty who can reason synthetically, for one who can reason analytically.*

[Note: Sherlock Holmes may have been a fictional character, but the author, Sir Arthur Conan Doyle, accurately predicted WWI, the method of submarine warfare that Germany would use, and campaigned for the building of a tunnel under the English Channel; all years before the outbreak of WWI.]

When I was a kid in school, I had trouble with math tests. Don't get me wrong, I was reasonably good at math; the problem was on tests you needed to show your work. I didn't do math as I was taught; I did it in my head. Now I was no prodigy (well, maybe an idiot--not a savant) by any means, but my thought processes gave me a different approach to problem solving (in fact, my wife is constantly reminding me I don't think like "normal" people). Years later, while in a computer school in the Navy, my instructors were describing how digital computers solved math problems by a process called "successive approximation". Eureka! That's pretty much how I did it. It was a simpler, faster, and more linear way to do math; at least it is for computers--and me. That is also why I really thrived in Boolean Algebra (logical and linear thinking), and why I struggled mightily in Calculus (non-linear--at least to my way of thinking). I only mention this to show there can be (for some of you), an easier approach to coming up with solutions to problems,

Top-Down Design, Thinking-Backwards, Analytical Thinking, they are all the same thing. It is the method used by all Investigators when solving criminal cases, and Engineers when "reverse engineering". The problem is--it should be used by everyone in analyzing (and solving) nearly everything, but is not.

When I talk about Design, I'm not just talking about what an engineer, architect, or a fashion designer does. We all design every day. We design solutions, strategies, business plans, marketing plans, advertisements, widgets, our living spaces, work processes, etc. Design, in this context is synonymous with problem solving and/or analysis. At the risk of being redundant, it bears repeating; it is the same process that detectives use to get to the truth and solve their cases. The much used phrase, "follow the money" is a perfect example of Top Down, Backward, or Analytical thinking.

I like to call this process Top-Down Design only because that it is easier for me, because of my technical background, to visualize. Again, calling it Thinking Backwards, Analytical Thinking, or Top-Down Design, it doesn't matter--as it is all the same thing. My approach to designing or analyzing anything is ass-backwards from most people. I always work backwards, or as I like to call it; Top-down. I prefer to follow the path of least resistance.

Which is easier and faster: climbing up a mountain, or falling down a mountain? It's falling down the mountain (TOP-DOWN), of course. If you are relating this to pain, that is entirely another issue. How many of you when solving a maze puzzle, start at the finish and work backwards to the start? I do, because it is easier and faster. At the beginning of a problem to solve, the options to choose from are more numerous and less clear than they are at the finish.

The first thing a successful Field Commander does when developing a strategy is to analyze the enemy and look for his target's weaknesses, and then works backwards from there, assigning the resources at his disposal to attack or counter-act the enemy's weaknesses. He does not first see what his own resources are, and then start the attack, A successful attack will be dictated by the weaknesses found in the opponent plans. (See how Design, and Strategic Thinking work together?)

A "Rube Goldberg" design (unless it is an intentional artistic statement) is a result of "climbing the mountain". Faced with a seemingly infinite array of ways to start, you just pick one. Which in turn may lead into a blind alley you have to backtrack out of, wasting valuable time. Then you pick another direction, and after a few convoluted twists and turns you find you are headed in an unrelated direction. Eventually most will get to the end, but along with wasting an extraordinary amount of time, it also expends an equally large amount of resources. The number of steps taken and/or developed processes to reach the end can become multiple rungs in the progress ladder. However, if you start at the objective you will see only a couple options open to you to get the desired result. This takes you down one rung on the progressive design ladder. From there you will see more clear and best options open to choose from, thus taking you down another rung. Eventually you will arrive at the starting point with a solution that is simple and efficient, with the fewest steps possible in the shortest amount of time. It's the path of least resistance; and, being an incorrigible couch potato, I am all for that.

Once when I was in a computer programming class, we were given a relatively simple programming task to accomplish. I did it in five or six lines of code, and I was done in about three minutes (I said it was simple). Some students were still writing and erasing after forty-five minutes. The professor had some of us go to the blackboard (pardon moi--Chalkboard--this was a long time ago, after all) to write our code out so it could be critiqued. A couple of us had very compact code, a few more had at least double and triple the amount of code, and one person took up a whole wall... Those others were examples of a bottom-up, non-linear design process.

When I was a Test Manager at GTE Information Systems, we needed a way to test the ASCII keyboards we manufactured. An engineer went off to his office and wasn't seen again for nearly a month. After a couple of days I got tired of waiting and got a hobby circuit board, some LED's, resistors, two or three small IC's, wire and connectors, and made-up a tester in an afternoon. It wasn't pretty, but it worked well and more importantly, it was extremely cheap and compact. A month later the engineer proudly showed up with a box, 10 inches to a side, and crammed full of expensive circuitry. It worked, and the complexity was impressive. Notice I said the complexity, and not the design. The design was cumbersome and anything but elegant. It was large, very expensive, and more prone to failure.

When I was a Field Engineer with Everett/Charles on my own time I designed a hand-held logic analyzer that was about six inches long, four inches wide, and one inch deep. The circuitry consisted of (if I remember right) eight small-scale IC's, and cost about fifteen dollars to make. A volume manufacturer could have produced it for three or four dollars, or less. It could monitor up to twenty electronic nodes of your choosing for a pattern you told it to look for (no matter how fleeting). Then, at that instant it would capture and display the instantaneous logic status of up to eight other electronic nodes, no matter how fleeting. Multiple units could be ganged together in order to double or triple the specs. Logic analyzers from Tektronix or Hewlett Packard cost many thousands of dollars (at the time) and were quite complex machines. My design was a result of "top-down-design". The extra benefit of this simple "top-down design" was it worked the first time; including the printed circuit board artwork (no debugging, or engineering changes needed). As a side note: I showed the prototype to an engineer friend in Delco (Kokomo), who got excited and wanted to show it to some people. So, I left it with him. A week later he called me and told me a group of doctors in Indiana wanted to invest in it, but under the condition they received a controlling interest of the company. My enormous ego got in the way. I, not knowing I couldn't do everything myself, turned them down. I viewed myself as another Steve Jobs or Bill Gates (my heroes and perceived peers). Now I would take the offer in a heartbeat. Forty-nine percent of somethin' mucho big is beaucoup better than one hundred percent of nothin'.

A few evenings before I left my Field Engineer job at Everett/Charles, I went out to dinner and drinks with our Engineering Manager. He wanted to know why our loaded-board "shorts and opens tester" was not selling. I told him it was only good for checking for solder-shorts and open circuits. Because there were a whole lot of other manufacturing induced problems, as well as "short and opens" which could be diagnosed on the larger more expensive testers on the market, there was no need for ours. He was disappointed until I said, "But you can make ours do nearly all those other testers can and at no extra cost. All it requires is a different perception of what you have, and a slight change to the software". I told him we currently test for 'shorts and opens' by applying a DC voltage across two nodes, and wait a prescribed amount of time before measuring the voltage to compensate for gross node-to-node circuit capacitance and impedance. Then reverse the nodes and do the same thing again. This gives you an indication of a short or open after compensating for the circuit resistance, junction direction, and capacitance. But, in addition to those capabilities, instead of waiting for the charge-time of the capacitance to be over, we could make two very quick voltage measurements during the charge time and record the results. Then make a final measurement once any capacitance has been compensated for. Then you reverse the polarity and do it again. Not only will this give you shorts and opens, but also the nodal charge slope. The end result is a function of net resistance and capacitance between those nodes, as well as any semiconductor junction direction present. This can be translated into verification of not only shorts and opens but also indicate the proper components of the proper values are present and properly oriented. And that is more than 95% of what the bigger more expensive testers can check for at a fraction of the cost and time. The last 5% of faults is the functionality of the components, which can be covered by the customer buying pre-tested components or testing them at "receiving inspection."

The next day it was announced Everett/Charles would have a "new tester" (Manufacturing Defects Analyzer) for sale within a couple of months.

The way I had approached it was to decide what I wanted to measure, and how I would manually check for those defects using my brain and a simple ohmmeter (and lots of time). Then, because I had developed and taught the technician classes on the tester I knew what the tester did. It was basically a computer-controlled ohmmeter with a very large switch matrix (substituting for arms). By reprogramming the software it improved its fault coverage capability about nine hundred percent. No one else in the industry had ever come up with that kind of tester. Honest.

A few weeks later, when I was working for Schlumberger, I had a near repeat of this previous scene with the Product Manager of their "loaded board shorts-tester" that competed with that of Everett/Charles. I gave him the same explanation-- with the same results. Yeah. De-ja-vu, all over again.

Now to someone reading this who is not electronics savvy, the previous paragraphs were probably just so much gibberish and gobbledygook. But, to those of you who are electronically literate, you probably said to yourself, "So what, that's obvious." You are right; it IS obvious (so obvious that it wasn't thought of by anyone else). That's the point. When you practice "top-down design", the solution or end result, will always be simple, efficient, and obvious. But, since most people don't design "top-down", it is the obvious solution that is rarely discovered. Notice the similarity here to Strategic Thinking. Know your enemy (the desired increased capabilities), and know yourself (how the existing tester did what it did). That ol' Sun Tzu keeps raising his wise 2500-year-old head.

Again, "top-down design" is nothing more than starting at the end, and then deciding on the easiest and most efficient way to accomplish the last step first. Then you back-up one step in the design and choose the easiest and most efficient way to accomplish that step. Then you repeat again until you arrive at the beginning. This is a guarantee the design (or, solution to the problem) is as efficient and effective as possible, and is accomplished in the fewest possible steps. Complex designs or solutions are inherently more problematic. (Microsoft bloatware comes to mind).

The top-down approach to problem solving makes it easier to break down, and understand or solve problems that we encounter every day.

One other thing; it also helps to make you "spin resistant"… Uh, did I already mention that I detest "spin"? In other words, you'll more easily see through other people's BS, and then you'll be left wondering why you're the only one who does.

The ability to analyze from the top down, or backwards, contributes to one's Competence, and makes Strategic Thinking easier and quicker.

'Analytical Thinking' (Top Down Design) also happens to be the second leg of the three-legged platform that is Leadership (competence), the first leg being Strategic Thinking. Next up is the third and final leg of the Leadership platform--'Ethical Thinking'.

Chapter 5

Ethical Thinking

This chapter will be blessedly brief. There will be no personal anecdotes, but be forewarned, as you may have already noticed, I can get preachy.

Sun Tzu: *The **Commander** stands for the virtues **of wisdom, sincerity, benevolence, courage and strictness.***

And… *The **Consummate Leader** cultivates the moral law, and strictly adheres to method and discipline; thus it is in his power to control success.*

Mark Twain: *Always do right. This will gratify some people and astonish the rest.*

Hippocratic Oath: *I will prescribe regimens for the good of my patients according to my ability and my judgment and **never do harm to anyone**.*

I had quite a difficult time coming up with the title for this chapter. I knew what I wanted to say, but I couldn't come up with a word that accurately reflected it. My choices were Right Thinking, Moral Thinking, and Ethical Thinking; but the problem is all three choices reflect relative behaviors. Politicians based on their political affiliation have commandeered Right Thinking; what is right for one party is not considered right for the other, and vice-versa. Those who are (or proclaim to be) religious have usurped Moral Thinking. Or, within those same sects, if one faction does not believe exactly as another faction there can be a conflict over what is moral or not moral. Doctors and Lawyers have some very different--and opposing--ideas as to what is ethical. So, I decided to redefine the term Ethical Thinking to more closely reflect my intent (and to leave no "wiggle room") by incorporating the sentiments of the aforementioned quotes.

Ethical Thinking: To consistently consider how one's actions can negatively affect others; always do right, be honest, and when possible try to do no harm...**Larry's New Standard Dictionary.**

That is much easier to say than to do. You can't always be honest when secrecy is legitimately needed for the good of the whole. For instance, our political leaders should not release military or intelligence information that can harm our military or intelligence sources; but some of them do. We may have to harm some people in order to protect the vast majority of our own people. To adequately take care of our poor, we may have to lean on the rich more; not make them poor as well, but just expect and require more help from them.

I can't stress enough how followers should always judge their leaders and potential leaders by these criteria. As President Reagan said, "Trust, but verify". If the followers would do that we would not be constantly surprised by our elected political leaders sudden exposures as being vain, venal, corrupt, immoral or unethical. We tend to ignore the signals we receive when the politicians say something we agree with. Not only that, but we frequently ignore what our political candidates have said or done in the past, and trust what they say in the present as long as what they are currently saying tickles our fancy.

One thing that just "frosts my balls" is when our leaders have "plausible deniability", willfully blind or ignorant, if you will, as opposed to stubbornly stupid. You know--when they do something illegal, or stupid, and have someone else under them take the blame, or "fall on their sword " like the John Edwards BS, or the Richard Nixon nonsense. Closely related to that is when a politician gets caught red-handed doing or saying something wrong, their first, second, and third response is to deny, deny, deny. They don't believe they are strong enough to survive an error (the corrupt probably aren't). Nixon probably would not have had to resign if he would have immediately accepted responsibility and apologized. Clinton wouldn't have had to go through what he did if he would have come clean and said "I'm sorry--I'm a horn-dog--but my sex life is my private business and not yours--butt out". John Edwards political career might have survived had he not lied about his mistress and child by having his underling claim the child was his.

*'When they call the roll in the Senate, the senators do not know whether to answer 'present' or 'not guilty.'...***Teddy Roosevelt**.

It was quite funny to watch the expressions on the faces of both Nancy Pelosi and John Boehner when the TV correspondent from '60 Minutes' nailed them about insider trading at a couple of unrelated press conferences. They were so surprised for a few seconds their lips were moving, but no sound was coming out.

In politics, religion, business or whatever, almost nothing is ever as it seems. The lack of honesty or real ethics (by my definition) is appalling.

Don't be sanctimonious or self-righteous, and don't follow those who are--either; it's not inclusive, and is always a dead end. Sanctimonious and self-righteous are terms that could have been applied to Elliot Spitzer, Reverends Tilton, Jim Baker, Jim Jones, and David Koresh.

Unfortunately, even though this is the shortest chapter, it is also the only one that I can't be of much help with regard to your ethical compass. Ethics is a sliding bar. One may have to lie in order to uncover the truth. Or, one might have to harm a few in order to help many; and who is to decide if the many are deserving, or if those same few are less deserving, or if the concept of deserving is even applicable? I'm obnoxious and opinionated, but I don't know. I only know I try to treat other people the way I wish to be treated (the Golden Rule). I can even see where in some circumstances it is even appropriate to do unto others BEFORE they do unto you. Hitler, Stalin and Mao were good candidates who easily come to mind.

Remember a few chapters ago when I said the people who say "Listen to me" and "Trust me" are pushing an agenda on you?

Well, **listen to me! Trust me!** See? I also have an agenda; and that agenda is to get people *to "Trust but verify"* **(Ronald Reagan).** Think about, and check out **everything** you hear and read, including what I'm writing or saying. Trust anyone you want, but **verify everything** that you hear or read so that you don't find yourself knee deep in doo-doo after following some idiot up a creek of you know what (Please pardon my mixed metaphor).

Finally, for all you budding, wannabe leaders, as well as those of you who prefer to follow, I'm ending with two quotes that everyone should live by, and, unfortunately, is observed by a paltry few (including me).

Never argue with a fool. Onlookers may not be able to tell the difference... **Mark Twain.**

99

*Never argue with a fool, they will drag you down to their level, and beat you with their experience every time...***Author unknown--frequently attributed to Mark Twain, but it's not.**

If you stand on the three legged leadership platform, and any one of those three legs (Strategic Thinking, Analytical Thinking, and Ethical Thinking) is weak or missing, your position as a leader is tenuous at best.

Whoa!!! Did you see that??? I just tied it all together! **I do love it when a plan comes together.**

Prior to the last crash of the stock market I was a "buy and hold", couch potato investor. After losing about 80% of my stock value in the crash I belatedly decided to learn how the stock market worked; how the pieces fit together; who was blowing smoke, and who was lying. Over the next three years, while learning and making horrendous and costly mistakes in the process, I was able to still average just a little over 100% return per year.

After writing this section I realized I was not following my own advice by taking this strategic approach to analyzing and investing in the stock market. So, I decided to *"Carpe mi sum Diem"*, and practice what I preach. Think about that one; don't gloss over it. *"Carpe* me some *Diem"*, come on, that's funny--right??? Well, at least I think it's the funniest thing I ever said, or wrote. Anyway, I then implemented it in my approach to investing in the stock market.

Since I track close to 70 stocks daily, I chose the 6 stocks that looked the most promising, and then took a few weeks to do an exhaustive analysis of each of those 6 stocks to determine the potential, as well as predicting individual events and results, identifying what can go wrong, and lastly identifying each unique investment strategy based on the benchmark events. Then I picked the one that looked the most interesting, and put some money in it. The result was I doubled my investment in 90 days. To re-quote Hannibal Smith, *"I love it when a plan comes together"* (I do love that quote). The act of watching a strategy play out as planned is as much fun as the actual results, and the "warm-and-fuzzies" last much longer.

Oh, yeah, one last thing. At the beginning of the Leadership chapter I mentioned nearly all my supervisors have told me that I'm a "natural leader". Am I? Nah! I just make an effort to be very competent. Many people have followed me because I was the only competent person around, and they didn't really have an intelligent alternative. I am quick-tempered, obnoxious, frequently pedantic (not to be confused with the word pedophile), and absolutely intolerant of stubbornly stupid--or the proudly ignorant. If you're ignorant of something I only give you a limited number of chances (and explanations) before I dismiss you entirely as a completely irretrievable idiot. I believe while everyone is **entitled** to their own opinion, they are also **obligated** to be as accurate and correct as possible in their publicly expressed opinion; otherwise, keep your idiot opinion to yourself. Remember, if you remain silent others may not find out just how stupid you really are. So no, I'm not a natural leader; I'm just pretty competent in some specific areas, with a burning desire to neither lead nor follow others, and a strong mistrust of people who think of themselves as leaders. My competence takes me up, and my personality and intransigence takes me out.

While this book is about leadership and what it takes to make (or judge) a good leader, it is really about encouraging people to think and use their reasoning ability instead of just being a parrot. A parrot may recite the Preamble to the Constitution, but that doesn't mean it understands what it is reciting.

I'm sorry, there is one final thing I feel that I must say. Regarding my anecdotes of insubordination while in the Navy, the point was not that I was prone to insubordination (I was, but only in the face of dangerous incompetence); the point was that I had some really piss-poor leaders, and I refused to follow them blindly. That is the moral for you followers; never--**ever**-- put your blind trust in **anyone**. Judas goats can lead you to the slaughterhouse with good intentions, or they can lead you to the slaughterhouse with evil intentions, but the end-result is still the same; you end up in the slaughterhouse (or, up a creek--knee deep in doo-doo) either way.

Actually, now that I think about it, I'm sure I would have made a damn fine dictator--albeit one with a very short life expectancy.

But wait (the man on TV says) there's more!!! (Bonus Material)

Next--the Search for Uncommon Sense.

In this next section are my thoughts on various issues that we run into everyday. I had published them in my Blog **'Musings From A Moderate'** that was posted on the Internet in 2010, and has since been discontinued and deleted. If you have found any nuggets of wisdom at all so far, read on at your own risk; it might result in enlightenment, or you may just need some Pepto-Bismol.

Subjects included are: politics, finance, the economy, healthcare, fair tax. Wall Street reform, immigration, the on-going recession, and (more importantly) the possible solutions for all of these problems.

Remember! You may come up with different solutions to the problems discussed. That's all right—as long as you arrive at them with reasoned thought based on empirical evidence and not anecdotal evidence or opinion. Don't trust what I say, but check it out for yourself. Use that Strategic, Analytical, and Ethical thinking you just read about and you'll be on the right track regardless of your conclusions.

Oh, yeah, the reason the Blog has been discontinued is that it was targeted toward moderates; and as we all know (or should know) moderates don't pay much attention to political discourse.

You may notice a difference in the tone and grammar. Here is an email from my brother.

"Attached is your book edited as of yesterday and all cleaned up for a clean read. I started the 'blog' portion and that is a different type of edit. Your book portion is getting information across to the reader. That makes it subject to proper English, spelling, grammar and syntax. The blog portion is your stated opinion and an edit there similar to the book portion could take away the punch factor your blog has. The best comparison would be if someone edited Yogi Berra or Archie Bunker."

I'm not sure whether I have just been complimented, insulted, or what, but the rest of the book is my exact words and punctuation, for better or worse, warts and all. I guess I will let the Archie Bunker and Yogi Berra in me shine through.

Part 2 In Search Of Uncommon Sense

Musings From A (Militant) Moderate

(First published in 2010, and updated, where appropriate, in 2012 and 2013)

A Political (and also not so political) discourse from the militant political middle.

I'm right, and you're probably wrong, unless, of course, you agree with me, in which case you're all right, and really smart! (Tongue is firmly in cheek)

By way of introducing myself (politically), let me say that--I am a moderate. That's not a confession, like I'm an alcoholic or something; that's a proud statement. I know; to both conservatives and liberals alike, that makes me wishy-washy, an unfortunate soul who can't make up his mind. Hogwash... It is that (like most of the people of this country) I don't view everything as black or white; I see everything as if it were a mosaic. That is, the proper "big picture" is made up of elements (both black and white, conservative and liberal) resulting in a "big picture" made up of infinite shades of gray.

If you were to plot out the American populace's attitudes about each question (both political and non-political) that impacts our lives, you would get a Gaussian plot similar to the one below.

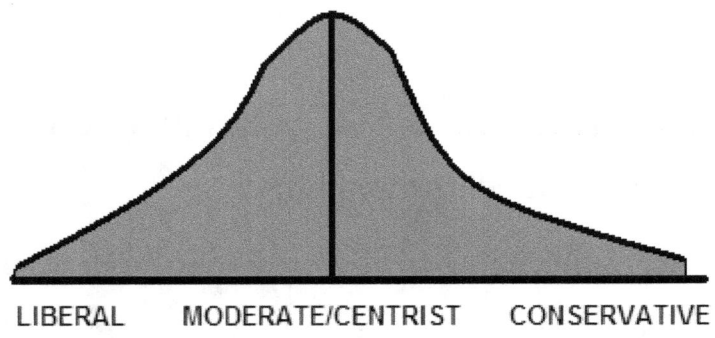

LIBERAL   MODERATE/CENTRIST   CONSERVATIVE

This plot would be the same regardless of the question. The more extreme liberal viewpoints tend to the left, the more extreme conservative viewpoints tend to the right, and the less radical viewpoints are clustered around the middle. A rational and thoughtful person does not have opinions or beliefs that are **exclusively** conservative or liberal

I recently heard a description that is apropos: Both extreme Liberals and extreme Conservatives are **Narrow Minded Nut Jobs!** They're Wing Nuts!

The people at either extreme are slaves to their rigid ideology, and are unable (or unwilling) to entertain any other ideas or positions. No sense letting facts and reason get in the way of a good hard-on. Of course, they don't see themselves as being rigid; they're just right. Many of the people just inboard from the extreme right or extreme left are not slaves to an ideology. Those people do, however, tend to come by their opinions by parroting people they respect, trust, or admire, much like children parrot their parents. They are simply "Toadies" for both the Right and Left. The remaining people in the middle (the true vast majority) are people who tend to expend a little more effort in coming up with their own thought out, reasoned positions.

It is not unusual to find a moderate person that has very conservative views regarding security or defense, but he/she can also have liberal social attitudes about, let's say, homosexuality, or abortion, or the death penalty. The reverse can also be true of a person with liberal attitudes who might at the same time feel uncomfortable about the extent welfare is extended to people. That's OK! Regardless of a person's viewpoint, if you have examined all the facts and elements before coming to a conclusion, it is an **informed** conclusion, and is the right one for you.

The point is a rational person will plot differently as their **thoughtful** opinion and conscience dictates for each subject.

That is why you will occasionally see some Democrats vote on the side of Republicans, and vice-versa. Anything else is dangerously one-dimensional. Notice I use the terms rational and thoughtful. These terms cannot be applied to the extremists on the right or the left (they really are two sides of the same coin, after all), or the verbal bomb throwers such as Rush Limbaugh, Sean Hannity, Ann Coulter, James Carville, etc. When they are not preaching to their constituency, these bomb throwers are actually quite thoughtful and intelligent. But, when they are "ON" in front of their fans, they are reactionary, rhetorical, and prone to inflammatory speech exciting (and inciting) their followers. Unfortunately, it is just these bomb throwers many people look to for guidance. These bomb throwers, and their slightly less extreme talking head counterparts on television and in the newspapers, are the ones from whom we get very biased information that we, as a population must use to form our opinions. These people could not care less about facts (I repeat, no sense letting facts get in the way of a good hard-on), they have an ideological agenda to put forward, and--ALWAYS--spin the facts in such a way as to support it. If they don't have facts to spin, they may make up something that is plausible, because they know that their fans do not have either the time or inclination to check up on their accuracy. They are fanatics, and because they are fanatics, consistency in logic is not a serious requirement among them. Both the conservatives and liberals sing the same "spinners" theme song (Half-Truth Boogie).

(Sung to the tune of 'Boot Scootin Boogie)

No matter I'm right--don't matter I'm wrong.

I spin all the facts--just to fit my song.

Get their heads a spinnin' like a big-ol hurricane.

I see everyone a-listenin' and believin' in me,

Cause my vision is all they're ever gonna see

While I go on a-singin' the Half-Truth Boogie,

Yeah the Half-Truth Boogie.

OK, I admit I'm not a songwriter. But the message is clear even though the song sucks.

I do not put Bill O'Reilly in the bomb thrower category. He is, indeed, an opinionated bully on the TV and radio, but his positions are always well thought out and supported, regardless whether you agree with him or not.

Always keep in mind a statement attributable to the fictional Sherlock Holmes, **"I have no data yet. It is a capital mistake to theorize before one has the data. Insensibly, one begins to twist facts to suit theories, instead of theories to suit facts."** A good example of this is the recent (2010), and ongoing brouhaha over health-care reform (Obama-care).

111

From the left our liberal leaders kept telling us reform would go a long way toward alleviating the problems associated with getting adequate healthcare to a very large portion of our population. They say the right-wingers want to withhold healthcare from the poor--so as to keep healthcare exclusive to those who can afford it (health does, after all, rhyme with wealth). The assault from the conservatives claimed it was a politically motivated attempt by the liberals to take over healthcare and expand government, and would also result in **nobody** getting decent healthcare. You may notice neither side could (or would) ever spout one single unbiased feature or fact of any bill that accurately supported their position. That is because while the need for healthcare reform may have had altruistic beginnings, the political process hijacked the argument. No one had seen any bill in question prior to voting, because it was a work in progress until the last moment. Even then it was not submitted to the full body of both houses for debate or vote; it was fast-tracked to the president. Even after the bill was finished you can bet not one Senator or Representative had bothered to read a bill that was in excess of two thousand pages. That's more than twice as long as a Steven King novel, and less entertaining. Who needs to have facts get in the way of a good, all out, political fight???

We do!

If you think about all **national** elections held you would notice that the candidates that plot closest to the center nearly always win. That is because in the absence of the occasional truly inspiring candidates like Roosevelt and Reagan, we hold our collective noses and vote for the lesser of two evils (being the right and the left), and regardless of which side you plot out on the graph, those of us in the center half are very uncomfortable with people who plot on either the far left or far right. The reason that I am bringing this up is that our political system is broken. The extremists from the far right and left have commandeered the two parties.

There are very few statesmen in politics at the national level, just--for the most part, corrupt opportunists.

When I say corrupt, I am not referring to being on the take (although there is plenty of that going on). No, I am referring to our elected representatives who are little more than a voting mouthpiece for special interests, because that is where the money (and votes) comes from so that they can spend enough to get re-elected to their cushy, lucrative, and powerful positions. There are a few statesmen in elected office (the blue dog democrats, and the moderate republicans, like Snow, and McCain, as well as a few independents like Lieberman), but they are greatly outnumbered, and get an unconscionable amount of verbal abuse heaped on them by both the right and left. What is their offense? They vote their conscience and belief, and they do not toe their party lines. We are currently being pulled apart by the dictator-like attitudes of both the extreme liberals and extreme conservatives in control of both of the parties, each wanting to dictate their agenda to everyone else.

The problem with dictators is that you can have either a benevolent rule, accompanied by great progress and enlightenment; or, just as easily, you can have a malevolent rule, with the accompanying suffering and injustices. **James Fennimore Cooper wrote**, *"The tendency of democracies is, in all things, to mediocrity"*. One can interpret this as meaning that if we all work together (with the accompanying compromise) we *may not* shine in enlightenment, but we (by the same token) also *will not* suffer.

Until we bolster the middle with access to moderate, or, God forbid, unbiased views and opinions, there will be no opportunity to start a moderate party, or, at least take back our existing parties from the self-absorbed extremists, and put into public office statesmen who dance to the strings being tugged by our needs instead of the pull of the special interests. The problem with being a moderate is that moderate people, for the most part, are neither loud nor noisy **(except for me--I'm both)**, and are also not activists. We tend to grouse about to ourselves, and to a few of our like-minded friends, and not ague with the obnoxious and sometimes vicious loud clowns with repugnant attitudes from either the right or the left **(again--except for me).**

Later in this Blog, you will see that **virtually all the problems** in this country are as a result of *special interests* getting *special consideration* from Congress and our Presidents.

To my wife's horror, as I age I am still a moderate, but I am no longer temperate.

Now we come to the reason for this Blog... I was a republican until a few years ago, but I now consider myself as an independent (registered as a Republican) because the Republicans are no closer to representing my beliefs than are the Democrats. I am not a Libertarian, mind you, Libertarians are just one step above anarchists, but I am a moderate independent. As moderates, we are in dire need of a source for an unbiased (or only slightly biased) reasoned view of the things and events that are affecting us. We need someone to cut through the biased BS that comes out of Washington and the talking heads on TV. While I have never called into a radio program, or written a letter to the editor, I am disgusted enough with what has been going on to say, "enough", and start doing this on my own. So, I'm like the guy that yelled (in the movie 'Broadcast News'), *"I've had enough, and I'm not going to take it anymore".*

In future postings to this blog, I will be looking at such subjects as the need for a "third party", the stimulus package, and, of course, health-care reform, the cause of our recent and ongoing recession, the need for Wall Street regulation, immigration, welfare, tort reform, and anything else that pops its ugly head up (like playing 'Whack-a-Mole'). Heck! If I get really nervy, I may even tackle religion. Wait--cancel that--I'm not going there. I guess that I'm going to post about whatever subject ticks me off after listening to the days talking (empty?) heads, and our political (puppets?) leaders. But the main thing is, I will be discussing things not from an ideological point of view, but from an examination of the facts and elements before coming to logical conclusions, at least--within my own morality and sensibility.

When I encounter people with extreme viewpoints that cannot be backed-up with logic or facts--I always hear them say, **"Everyone has a right to their own opinion."** To which, I respond, **"Yes, you do, indeed, have a right to your own opinion, but you also have an *obligation* to be correct."** Then they look at me like I am speaking Swahili, so I change the subject. They're just another narrow-minded nut job; either profoundly ignorant or stubbornly stupid.

This last paragraph is going to be repeated at the end of every single one of my posts because it bears keeping in mind.

The purpose of our government (and the people who are employed by our government) can be summed up by a sign, which I saw on a police car in California, *"To protect, and to serve"*. To that, I would like to add one word *"-everyone"*. Not just the rich at the expense of the poor, or the poor at the expense of the rich, not the powerful at the expense of the weak, or vice-versa. Our government exists *"To protect, and to serve – everyone"*. And if that means compromise--so be it.

Chapter 6

Let's Have A Party

A third party--that is.

Our government has become, over the last 40 years, so polarized because of the take-over of both the Democratic and Republican parties by the extreme left and the extreme right, that we are in a near permanent state of "grid lock". On the one hand, gridlock is good; it prevents our leaders from doing any real harm to us because of their "mandate" or "vision". But, on the other hand, gridlock also has the effect of preventing our leaders from improving our lives, or even protecting us.

Both of the extremes (liberal and conservative) have views of the world--and the way it should be, which are polar opposites. These extreme views do not allow them to work together to solve our problems except in extreme emergencies such as after 911. The extremists in either camp have no interest in serving the best interests of everyone; they are interested only in serving the interests of their ideology, and their constituency. In their desire to gain (or regain) power so that they can force their ideology on everyone they have decided to obstruct, at every opportunity, their political opposites. What do you get? Gridlock.

If you look at a two-partner business as a model you can easily see why the two-party system does not work.

Here are the three possible scenarios and their dynamics:

1. Equal Two-Party Partnership: That is, each partner has 50% ownership and control, as a permanent status. This is the best option of the three, but still not a good idea. The only way that any decisions can be made is when both parties agree. The instant either party disagrees the decision automatically defaults to the side that is against the proposal. This works if both partners have moderate outlooks and put the interest of the company (or people) ahead of their own self-interest. This is what statesmen do, but not what politicians do, and we currently have too damn few statesmen serving us in our government. If either party acts only in his or her own self-interest, much needed progress will not happen causing the company (or country) to stagnate, and in some cases wither and die.

2. Unequal Partnership: This is when one partner has controlling interest, and thus whatever that partner wants-that partner gets--without regard to what the minority partner wants or needs, nor also whatever the company (country) wants or needs. This is suspiciously like that of another business/political entity; it is how both a sole proprietor ownership and a dictatorship operate. That is good if the true interests of the company or country is at heart, but a benevolent dictator can too easily become a malevolent dictator. That is when the interests of the individual take precedence over the interests of the company or country. While our government is not (in fact) a dictatorship, both parties, when they are in charge, act like an ideological dictatorship.

3. Managing Partner: That is when one partner is in permanent control, and the other partner is used as permanent support. This works the same as the second scenario. Can you imagine, in our government, the republicans willingly allowing the democrats to have total and permanent control? Or vice-versa? Never happen. There is no trust, and rightly so.

None of these three options is a very good idea.

Ideally what is needed is a partnership of more than two partners, and in which no one partner has controlling interest in the company or government. This doesn't guarantee that the interests of the company or country will be served, but the odds of that happening will be much better. A side benefit would be that there is much less likelihood of gridlock.

If you have a party of hard core liberals, a party of hard core conservatives, and a party of moderates sharing power, what you will get would be legislation that will benefit most Americans   instead   of legislation that benefits only the small demographics that are the favorites of either the extreme left or the extreme right. Neither faction would be able to force their very narrow-minded agendas down our collective throat.

One problem with starting a third party is that moderates are not activists. There is no fire in our belly's regarding ideology because moderates choose the best solution to fit the situation. We, as moderates, do not have a single ideology to push.

Another problem is leadership. Political parties need charismatic leadership. If you look at the few truly moderate politicians there are few that you can point to that excite you. That has been the case throughout history. Most of the charismatic leaders of both the past and present have been disasters. Think: Hitler, Lenin, Mao, Mussolini, and Khomeini, as well as Jim Jones and David Koresh. The thing in common with these Charismatics is that they were all extremists who excited their followers; at least--at first.

The last experiment with a third party (United We Stand) was with Ross Perot. He was quite a charismatic character that initially appealed to the moderates of both the Republican and the Democratic Parties, with common sense ideas. The problem was that he was discovered to be a flake. This caused the true moderates to abandon both him and the party to the flakiest remnant. If he wouldn't have turned out to be such a flake he might have actually won, or at least, might have changed the face of our political system for the better.

Our best shot is to encourage the "tea party" fans to make that a real political party. They have fire in their guts and the support from the extreme right of the Republican Party. This would give a political outlet to the extreme right, leaving control cf the Republican Party to the moderates. The Republican Party would then be an attractive place for the disaffected moderate Democrats to migrate to, leaving the liberals in control of the Democratic Party, as they already are.

We can only hope that the "tea party" group won't self-destruct like the Perot party did. Have you noticed the similarity between the tea party supporters, the later stages of the Perot-started party, and the radical demonstrations of the sixties? They all have, or had, a strong distrust of leadership (except their own), and are, or were, more or less libertarian with attitudes that fringe on anarchy.

At a minimum we need them to organize so that they can get the right wing, narrow-minded nut jobs out of the party in order that the moderates can regain control.

All this would marginalize both the hard core left, and the hard core right, but still would allow their valuable contributions to the political process. They both do, after all, have some good ideas; it is just that neither one is universally correct--and they both also refuse to believe that. We moderates would then be able to pick and choose the best ideas for the benefit of this country as a whole.

Well, I can dream, can't I?

How about forming a new party for moderates?

The problem with the alternative of abandoning the Republican Party to the narrow-minded nut jobs, and forming a new and moderate political party is that, as I mentioned before, moderates who have charisma and also have the burning desire necessary to start a new political party are hard (if not impossible) to find. When was the last time you saw a moderate person standing on a corner, holding a sign that says, *"The end is NOT near."*

Here it comes!

The purpose of our government (and the people who are employed by our government) can be summed up by a sign, which I saw on a police car in California, *"To protect, and to serve"*. To that, I would like to add one word *"-everyone"*. Not just the rich at the expense of the poor, or the poor at the expense of the rich, not the powerful at the expense of the weak, or vice-versa. Our government exists *"To protect, and to serve – everyone"*. And if that means compromise--so be it.

Chapter 7

Supreme Court Appointment

(My Blog during the search for the replacement for a retiring Justice.)

Here we go again. I'm going to start off with something I've said more than once to the politically active.

OK folks--take a breath!

The talking heads on TV and the conservative radio talk-show hosts (there are no liberal talk -show hosts) are trying to stir up controversy where there need be none.

The people who claim to represent the conservatives (who after all, according to them, are the majority) are already vilifying any POTENTIAL candidates for the Supreme Court who aren't an archconservative. The people who claim to represent the liberals (who also are the majority, aren't they?) are already pushing for the president to nominate someone that matches their ideology. We all know, according to the far right, that all moderate and liberal judges are just lackeys of the far left, who are closet crime-condoning, communist, big government, baby killer, income redistribution atheists, who want to legislate from the bench. And we all know, according to the far left, that the moderate and conservative judges are non-caring, gun toting Nazis, who can't stand progress, and want to trample over all our liberties (kill them all, and let God sort them out), and force their religion-du-jour down our throats. You know what? They're both right--kinda. There are elements of both the extremes that do exemplify many of those attitudes, but most do not. An extremist judge generally will not rise to national prominence. That is because on a national stage their idiocy is quickly recognized and they are ultimately marginalized.

That doesn't mean an extreme liberal "nut job" judge won't thrive in--say--San Francisco, or an extreme conservative "nut job" judge won't thrive somewhere in the deep south. They can, and do. They just are not tolerated outside of their localized area of support. Most judges and legal minds who are prominent on the national stage are moderates who rule according to the law, or their interpretation of the law. They don't stray too far in their interpretations, because they don't want to have their judgment be overturned (a very good way to screw up your judicial career).

With very few exceptions, there have been very few truly liberal or conservative acting Supreme Court Justices. That is why we have had judges that have been accused, by both the right and left, of being turncoats (traitors to their ideology). What they really are--are people who take their position and duties extremely seriously, and try to make all their decisions as intellectually honest decisions based on their individual interpretations. That is why they are paid well, and appointed for life. We do not want them to be influenced by anything but intellectual argument, and certainly not by political persuasion.

The issue of interpretation necessitates that I bring up the issue of those who promote "strict constructionists". That is, no interpretation at all, but that they should strictly follow the Constitution as it is worded.

That can't possibly work. The Constitution was written over two hundred years ago and is based on the realities of the time. Not only has the country moved on technologically, but also in regard to religion, and even language.

First lets take language as an example. The Second Amendment says that because of the need for a well-regulated militia, our citizens have the right to bear arms. Liberals like to point out the words "well regulated militia" as meaning that only the military and law enforcement should have arms, and any civilian use needs to be regulated very closely. The problem is that when the Constitution was written, the use of the term "well regulated" was frequently used to mean well outfitted (or, in this case, well armed), not well controlled. And militia was just a term for a civilian force that when banded together could withstand tyranny from both outside and inside our own country. A strict, and accurate interpretation would allow anyone to have any weapon they wish (in order to be well outfitted) to resist oppression. However, I know some people (I'm sure that you know some as well) whom I do not wish to see in possession of a machinegun or an RPG, and certainly not a Surface-to-Air Missile, or a Tank. This amendment has to be interpreted to follow its original intent, as closely as possible, without unduly endangering the rest of the population. And if you think about it, The Supreme Court, regardless of its conservative or liberal leanings, never strays far from that intent.

The changing of technology shows the need for interpreting the First Amendment. We have the freedom of speech--period. Not the freedom of televised controversial images. Not the unregulated use of email, radio, telephone, or the use of political donations by companies, labor unions, or PAC's. The First Amendment doesn't take any of those in consideration because they didn't exist when the Constitution was written. Of course, if we truly want strict interpretation of the Constitution we could still have all those things; they would just have to be subject to censorship by whoever is in power at any particular time because they are not expressly permitted in the Constitution. Also in the First Amendment we are guaranteed freedom of religion. The liberal left interprets that to also mean freedom FROM religion. The conservative right likes to point out that we have always had government references throughout our short history to the existence of GOD, and we are a Christian nation, so the government should give Christianity a little advantage.

The problem is that while our founding fathers wanted to protect the religious freedoms of the various sects of the Protestants, and Catholics as well as Jews, there were precious few Muslims, Hindu, Buddhist, Mormons, or Atheists, and certainly--no Scientologists in the early days of this country. Remember, the Constitution was written only 100 years after the Salem Witch Trials. This amendment is normally **interpreted** as not condoning state sponsorship or persecution of any religion. The jury is still out on how this amendment will continue to be interpreted, but odds are that it will continue to be interpreted as not promoting any religion at all in the interest of being inclusive of all spiritual beliefs, as well as lack of beliefs. This, believe it or not, is closer to that of a strict constructionist interpretation of the Constitution. One last nail in the "strict constructionist" argument is that the United States was set up so that each state was a sovereign entity, and the United States was kind of like NATO. That is, it is an association of like-minded sovereigns with common goals and freedoms banded together for mutual defense and commerce. That **interpretation** was permanently put to rest by the Civil War because of the propensity of the southern states to interpret the phrase in the Declaration of Independence *"all* *men are created equal"* as more along the lines of the book 'Animal *Farm'*, *"all men are created equal, but some are more equal than others"*.

Basically I have used a lot of words to say that, regardless who ultimately gets appointed, everything will be OK. And remember, the reason we have nine justices on the Supreme Court is that if we do accidentally get a narrow-minded nut job on the bench, the other eight Justices will marginalize him or her. The Justices, as a group, never stray too far from the middle.

And, again!

The purpose of our government (and the people who are employed by our government) can be summed up by a sign, which I saw on a police car in California, *"To protect, and to serve"*. To that, I would like to add one word *"-everyone"*. Not just the rich at the expense of the poor, or the poor at the expense of the rich, not the powerful at the expense of the weak, or vice-versa. Our government exists *"To protect, and to serve - everyone"*. And if that means compromise--so be it.

Chapter 8

How About A Fair Tax Plan For A Change?

(Written in 2010, but every few years these tired ideas keep being resurrected.)

A few days ago a friend of ours came home from a business trip with exciting news.

"Have you heard about the Fair Tax Plan?" he asked.

"You must have discovered Neal Boortz on the radio." I said.

He said, *"Yeah! You're familiar with it?"*

I said, *"Yeah! It's like all the other Fair Tax Plans that conservatives (and the rich) keep trotting out. It's Snake Oil."* My friend wasn't too enthused with my answer.

Now, I'm not picking on conservatives unfairly with regard to fair tax plans. It's just that it's mainly conservatives that want to cut taxes for their constituency--and have the ability to make the noise necessary to get public attention. Of course, moderates would like to have their taxes cut. But as I've said before, moderates are not driven by ideology and have no loud verbal bomb throwers on their side willing to trumpet their causes. And, of course, liberals never want to cut taxes. **Ever!** At least, not while there are still hundreds, nay, thousands of causes out there which have a need to be funded.

First off-- lets talk about "Fair".

Fair is a concept that is relative to the individual, or special interest, with regard to any issue.

Is it fair that 10% of the American population be looked upon to pay 90% of the income taxes? **Absolutely not!!** But it is equitable; about 90% of the income goes to that 10% of the population. It also shouldn't come as any surprise to you that approximately 90% of the property, equity, and wealth (by any definition), are also held by that very same 10% of the population. Like the old Gatlin Brothers song went, "All the gold in California--is in a bank--in the middle of Beverly Hills--in somebody else's name."

Is it fair that the top 10% of the earners pay 90% of the taxes? **No**, but it is equitable; and like the bank robber said when he was asked why he robs banks, *"Because that's where the money is."*

Is it fair that people with no school age children are required to pay school taxes, while those with vast herds of children get not only tax breaks on income tax, but can also get tax credits? No way! However, it is equitable! An educated populace is one of the things that have helped make this county what it is.

The only thing truly unfair is that school funding is tied to local property taxes. This allows wealthier neighborhoods to have very good public schools, while the conditions of schools in poorer neighborhoods are frequently absolutely deplorable. You get what you pay for. On the other hand, it does let us keep the riff-raff down. Who needs to give the uppity poor an even chance and delusions of grandeur (my tongue is firmly in my cheek folks, please don't nuke me)?

Is it fair that poor people who have a disproportionate number of fires in their homes, and who also utilize our police services disproportionately, aren't billed by the police and fire departments for the extra burden they place on our society, or that the people who never use those services aren't given an appropriate tax rebate reflecting their reduced burden on society? **Heck no, it's not fair!** In the larger view of things, though, it is equitable! It is what the concept of insurance is supposed to be, but isn't (that will be another rant, at another time), and that is to spread the cost so that those services are affordable to everyone.

One word that I have just used a number of times is a word that you will never see used with regard to the various fair tax plans--**Equitable!!!**

There have been a number of fair tax plans proposed over the years, and they all propose one or more of the following elements to replace the current graduated income tax.

1. Flat tax. Everybody pays the same percentage.

2. National sales tax.

3. National value added tax.

There is one thing to keep in mind when listening to these various fair-tax plans, and that is that they all are designed to reduce the tax burden on the wealthy. Now, if you reduce the burden on one segment, then you have to make a corresponding increase on some other segment in order to make up for the shortfall. There is no way around it. If you lower the taxes on one group, you must make up for the loss by doing one of two things. Either raise taxes on another group, or reduce services, both of which penalize the remaining groups.

Another thing in common is the sales pitch. Each proponent puts out a pitch of such a high quality, that they could each get rich selling time-shares. They spin out so many facts and figures, that it makes your head spin. They get you nodding and agreeing with their individual points, so that they get you to forget about the one fact that is important to you, and agree with them (an often used sales technique, by the way). That one fact is that the income tax for the wealthiest group of Americans would be less than it is now, and higher for everyone else.

Most of the people are sharp enough (when, and if, they take the time to think about it) to see the illogic of the flat tax schemes (both the flat percentage scheme, or a true flat tax, or more accurately--a head tax--which actually would be the fairest).

Why not a head tax?

Let's say a head tax of $10,000 per year were put on every man, woman, and child in America so that a single person would pay $10,000, a couple would pay $20,000, and a family of 7 would pay $70,000. Certainly, this is unworkable and inequitable, but is truly the fairest possible tax of all; a family of 7 also places 7 times the burden on society that a single person does.

Most of the plans now being trotted out are variations of the National Sales Tax, and National Value Added Tax plans.

That's where they can really get you into buying their BS. It sounds good and fair to have a sales tax or a value added tax because it affects everybody based on his or her consumption. Of course, they always talk about an exemption for the poor, because they know you can't squeeze blood from a turnip. There is one big flaw in those schemes, (at least from a moderate or middle class point of view), and it is the secret main attraction for the wealthy (and their conservative puppets). That is the fact that the wealthy do not spend all their income. The poor spend all their income; even most of the middle class spends all their income. Surplus income (the kind that allows the ability to make serious investments) only starts at the very upper middle class. The net result is that both of these tax plans result in less tax on the wealthy, shoving a bigger share of the tax burden onto the middle class.

Compare a middle class person that makes $50,000 per year, to one of the Wall Street crooks, I mean--uh--CEO's, that receives $50,000,000 per year, or 1,000 times as much. The middle class person probably spends nearly every penny of his income unless he is very frugal and is able to save a couple of thousand out of that amount, while the person making $50,000,000, might live quite extravagantly and spend $10,000,000, still allowing him to invest $40,000,000. This disparity allows the fat cat, who makes 1,000 times as much as the lower income worker, to pay only 200 times as much in consumption tax. This is a good illustration of the old saying about how the rich just keep getting richer.

I have repeatedly heard various conservative mouthpieces on financial programs on the radio and TV point out (with a great deal of indignation) that 40% of the population in the United States **does not pay ANY tax at all.** That's right, 40% of the population **doesn't make ANY money.** Heck 20-25% of the population is either unemployed, or under-employed.

This disparity is why supply side economics, or Reagan's trickle-down economics, doesn't work. The rich and their conservative mouthpieces know this, but it is not in their own best (short term) interest to acknowledge it. The liberals, who are too busy saving Whales, Spotted Owls, Snail Darters, and trees, and sending good money down rat holes, (did you ever notice that getting liberals to unite is like herding cats?) to think that deeply--in order to explain to the populace the trap that the conservatives are laying. Besides, liberals oppose these tax plans based on fundamental philosophy. That is that **those who make all the money--should pay all the bills**. From their standpoint--that's the name of that tune--end of that story.

While I'm on the subject of taxes, I'm going to launch into my favorite thing to rant about--tax cuts.

The Republicans, when faced with a slumping economy, yell, ***"Cut the taxes. It will stimulate job growth"***. Then, when the economy is booming they chant, ***"Cut the taxes. The economy is good, and there's no need to spend so much"***. Which is it? It doesn't work both ways.

The problem with cutting taxes in order to stimulate job growth is that tax cuts do not stimulate job growth. The need to produce more—stimulates job growth. It's all about supply and demand. Companies do not hire people because the pay less taxes. They **hire people in order to produce more products, or services,** from which they can then **generate**

137

more profits. World War II gave us a good lesson. Some of the highest taxes in United States history were during WWII. That is also a time when there was virtually no unemployment, and enormous wealth generation. That is paraphrasing a statement by Ben Stein, who may be familiar to you as the boring teacher at the beginning of the movie *'Farris Buhler's Day Off'*, or from his TV show *'Who's smarter than Ben Stein'*. He also is on the panel of mostly conservative financial pundits on the Fox News Channel, and was a speechwriter who has served presidents Nixon and Ford. His father was also a noted economist. Ben Stein is considered to be a conservative. But, after listening to him frequently I think that he is (although he may deny it) more of a closet moderate. Tax cuts actually have very little effect on the economy. Shortly after any tax increase the economy softens because companies and individuals slow down consumption while they figure out the new realities. Then, 12-18 months after the tax increases, the economy ALWAYS turns back up, in spite of the tax increases, because the companies and individuals have figured it out and start consuming again. I'm not making this up--check it out.

Now in today's rant I keep railing about "the wealthy" like I don't like them. Wrong!! I love them. I want to be one of them, and I don't begrudge any of them for wanting to get and keep more; that is only human nature. It is just that a well-informed and just public can, and should, look out for not only our own interests and well-being, but that of our neighbors as well. I am not going to try to define the level of income above which you are determined to be "wealthy". That is a task that has to be debated upon and decided by our representatives. Lets just say that the "wealthy' are those who have no problems affording high quality food, high quality shelter, high quality health care, high quality education, etc., and have enough money left over to save and invest so that they can accumulate enough in order to continue to experience an equally high quality life style after retirement. I know--I know, that was a long and clumsy sentence, but that's the best I can do. Sorry. Besides, a period is too precious a thing to waste.

There is one last pet peeve of mine. Whenever the rich start whining about needing a tax reduction, keep in mind that everything over a couple of hundred thousand dollars per year is exempt from Social Security tax (FICA). That is, they don t have to pay the 6.5% FICA tax that everyone below that threshold must (even the poor). Remember, FICA is a tax, not an insurance premium. And for those people who are self-employed, the advantage is doubled to 13%. Also, I've read that about 40% of the income in the U.S. is in the form of Capital Gains or unearned income (taxed at a much lower rate, and also not subject to FICA). And who has the lion's share of the Capital Gains? It sure as hell ain't the poor, or even most of the middle class.

[The following was added in 2012:

Warren Buffet proposed what I think is a very reasonable suggestion. That is to apply a minimum tax of 30% to ALL income over $500,000, regardless of the source (that means dividends, capital gains, whatever), and eliminate the deductions and loopholes for income over $500,000. I would like to modify that and see it go a step further by extending the FICA income cap to $500,000, or more, as well as keep the minimum tax rate at 35%, as it is now, and end the deductions and loop-holes only for all income over $500,000. Even under those conditions--those with incomes over $500,000 would still be taxed at an overall rate less than those with incomes under $500,000 because of the FICA disparity. Someone please get me a band-aid, **my heart is bleeding.**

Couple that with rational spending reductions in defense spending, sovereign welfare and corporate welfare, as well as curbing the abuses (well intentioned, or not) in public welfare, and we just may be able to straighten our fiscal mess out.]

Oh, Oh, here we go again!

The purpose of our government (and the people who are employed by our government) can be summed up by a sign, which I saw on a police car in California, *"To protect, and to serve".* To that, I would like to add one word *"-everyone".* Not just the rich at the expense of the poor, or the poor at the expense of the rich, not the powerful at the expense of the weak, or vice-versa. Our government exists *"To protect, and to serve – everyone".* And if that means compromise--so be it.

Chapter 9

Who's To Blame For The Recession?

Who's to blame for the recession?

In a word, **everyone**! There is enough blame to go around to touch nearly every person in the United States.

That's right. The Liberals are to blame. The conservatives are to blame. The moderates are to blame (our lack of drive, or laziness in oversight, allowed the crazies to gain control). The poor are to blame. The wealthy are to blame, and the middle class is to blame. Our political leaders are to blame, the people in charge of our financial institutions are to blame, and last but not least, our corporate leaders are to blame. Did I leave anybody out? If I did, it is just an unintentional oversight and you will probably see any omitted groups fingerprints somewhere in the following explanation of the elements that caused the recession and financial meltdown.

The recent financial meltdown and following recession resulted from a perfect storm of events that really would have been worse if many regulations enacted as a result of the great depression hadn't been in place. However, it probably wouldn't have been as bad, had our regulators and congressional overseers not relaxed or ignored some of the rules.

There are many events that led up to the meltdown. I will examine some of them one at a time, and it will be clear by the end of this post how it all fits together, and who is clearly to blame.

First, there was the monumental run up of oil prices that took trillions of dollars out of our economy. This is money that, had it still been in circulation, could have kept the nations economy running. But, as it was, it not only needlessly took money out of almost every persons pocket, but it made everything that was needed for us to survive to be much more expensive. It also made the normal conducting of business so much more costly that it, in some cases, made it unprofitable to continue. Thus the lay offs and business closures that made things worse.

Everyone wants to blame the "oil companies" and / or the "Arabs" for the price increases. But they may be the only innocent parties in this fiasco. The commodity markets set prices for **all commodities.** And, who sets the price of the commodities at the commodity markets? **We do,** not the "Arabs" or "Big Oil". The oil companies and OPEC just profited a great deal from the   gift that we gave them.

Commodity markets were started hundreds of years ago to help stabilize prices by making the commodities more liquid, and allow for producers to hedge their future positions in case the prices were not favorable. This was needed because of the old "supply and demand" theory. It used to be that there were not many customers for basic commodities, which led to tremendous price volatility. However, starting decades ago this was no longer the case. There are now hundreds of millions of customers who purchase or use most of the commodities, and so there are more than enough buyers to supply the liquidity and price stability needed. The reason that we still have the commodity markets is to provide another avenue for investors, gamblers, bankers and brokers to make money. Even so, it still worked fairly well up until about 10-12 years ago.

The reason that it worked was that commodity (futures) investing is very highly leveraged, making little price changes (and cash in accounts) turn into huge profits or losses. It is also very fast. A commodity investor has to monitor news-feeds and events, and be able to get in and out very quickly. This is not something that the average investor is capable of. This limited the number of participating investors, and also kept the number of contracts available in balance with potential investors. That is why, if the Saudi's said that they were going to cut oil production next month, the price went up in anticipation. Next month when they didn't cut production, but actually increased it, the price went down.

The law of "Supply and Demand" at work.

Sometime around 10-12 years ago the investment banks, brokerages, and exchanges wanted to tap into the huge group of investors that were staying out of commodities due to both risk and ability. They got our regulators to agree to allow them to create financial instruments that are traded like exchange-traded funds, only, instead of stocks--they were investments in commodity futures contracts. Not only that, but they were allowed to also create more highly leveraged instruments (of the already highly leveraged commodities contracts) that returned double and even triple the price increase (and loss) of the commodity price swings. Keep in mind all these institutions make money on the trade of these contracts, not the results of these contracts.

What resulted was that huge amounts of money started pouring into these instruments from the vast pool of investors that had previously been left out. This increased the demand for the limited number of contracts available, thus increasing the price. Now unlike the traditional commodities investor who changes or cancels his position due to supply and demand of the commodity, these instruments do not do that. If they are investments that buy contracts, that is all they do. They don't reverse their positions. That is done by a different instrument, and vice-versa. The result is that commodity futures (short shelf life) became an asset (long shelf life) class of investment. That is why the price continued to climb (irrationally) due to the supply and demand of the **contracts**, and not the fundamentals (the supply and demand) of the **underlying commodity**. Then, when it became obvious that the extraordinarily high price couldn't be maintained, the investors in these 'up" instruments all jumped on the corresponding "down" instruments. This created heavy pressure on the prices and drove them down like an elevator; but by then the damage to the economy had already been done.

What happened then, was that some of our political representatives finally started to notice, and began to talk about an "investigation". This caused Deutchebank to end its "double up--oil" (DXO) exchange traded note voluntarily, as it was seen as the most visible culprit. As a result the hearings and regulation reform never happened. That mollified congress, but the "double down oil" ETN was still allowed to exist, as well as the "single up" and "single down" instruments. That is why, even with over-supplies in oil and a reduction in demand, the price is still creeping up. It will continue to do so, only slower, until such time everybody with an up position jumps to the down side. Look at it as if it were a sightseeing boatload of passengers. Every one is looking on one side of the boat at the spouting whale, making the boat lean to that side nearly to the point of capsizing. Then, when the whale disappears and some seals are spotted on the other side, all the passengers stampede to the other side, nearly causing the boat to capsize to that side. This is the price volatility that the markets were designed to avoid; and it is that price volatility that will lead to future economic problems if not headed off by regulation. We need to end exchange-traded instruments that allow investments in commodities.

Now lets look at the most visible element of the meltdown. Housing!

Here, everyone gets blame. Liberals get blame for wanting to give "the poor" housing of their own that they couldn't otherwise afford (they are, after all, called poor for a reason). The liberals did this by twisting congresses arm to encourage the relaxing of the mortgage qualification rules for the very people that shouldn't ever get a mortgage. The conservatives should have put their foot down, but their vision was clouded by the huge short term profits to be made by themselves and the various lobby groups by including this huge (previously underserved) class of customers as home owners.

The funding for this experiment came from creating securitized-motgage bundles. They are bundles of mortgages that were then traded as if they were stocks. The resulting increased demand, and limited supply of the bundles, drove the prices higher--which increased the supply of capital--which made borrowing even cheaper--which increased the number of poor quality buyers--which resulted in increased real estate value--which made the investments look artificially safe. After all, who cares if there is a foreclosure when you can resell it for even more? Besides, we can make money now, and any possible risk is someone else's problem far out in the future.

While securitized-motgages were developed to "spread the risk", and Fannie Mae and Freddy Mac were only to produce and sell them; they started to believe in the very BS they were creating. They were supposed to only produce and sell these bundles in order to fund new mortgage bundles. However, they themselves started to accumulate these flawed financial instruments, which eventually made them insolvent when the prices inevitably collapsed.

All these financial institutions can be looked at as if they are book-making operations. That is, they make their money from handling the bet (or transaction), but no good book-making operation **ever** places a bet of their own. That's for suckers.

About this time regulators changed the accounting rules to value these mortgage bundles and other derivative investments as the price that they bring at the most recent auction, not what it was actually bought at, or the real underlying value. The reason for this was the inclination for many of these financial institutions to want the books to look better; and if the most recent auction values it more, well that just makes the books look even better. That seems reasonable, except when the real estate market started to collapse, the market for these bundles ceased almost overnight, making their official value essentially zero, while the real value was something quite a lot more. The resulting collapse made nearly all of the financial institutions either insolvent, or at least appear to be insolvent.

The rules that the banks used to live by, was that they could be leveraged 11 to 1. That means that they could owe eleven dollars for every dollar in asset value. Then the representatives in congress changed that so that the ratio was to go up to (I believe) 13 to 1. That was so that their fat cat buddies could make even more money. Then the really inexcusable thing that happened was that the regulators looked the other way while these "banks" went to as much as 50 to 1 or more. That alone made them technically insolvent, but as long as real estate was appreciating it didn't matter. When the market for these mortgage bundles collapsed almost overnight, nearly all the big banks were, in fact, technically bankrupt and insolvent. This ultimately resulted in the inability for them to make loans for business or for consumption. We will explore the ensuing bail out in another post.

One other thing contributed to the meltdown: AIG! We have all heard about AIG, but I am going to go over it briefly here.

AIG was selling insurance policies on the bonds and mortgage bundles that the investment banks were issuing, which would pay off in the event of default. These were the infamous credit default swaps (CDS), and credit default obligations (CDO). The reason that they have these weird names and were not just called insurance policies was that they were sold, and later traded to third parties, like bonds and stocks. This is not legal for insurance companies to do because insurance policies cannot pay-off to an uninterested third party who has no skin in the game. Because of this bogus naming of the insurance policies, regulators (who are supposed to be watching out for our interests instead of looking the other way) wouldn't have to look too closely and stop them. These policies flooded the market, and helped swell the assets of the various banks, funds, institutions and even countries. The collapse of the banks and mortgage bundles caused these insurance policies to be paid, but not necessarily to the entities that had the actual insured mortgage bundles that would take the hit on the loss. These insurance policies, as well as the mortgage bundles, were owned by people and institutions all over the world, and threatened to totally swamp the world economy if, as was the case, AIG couldn't make good on them.

You can see that we, as moderates, should have said no to the liberals who wanted to give something to "the poor" that they couldn't responsibly handle. We need to recognize that helping the poor and throwing money down a rat hole is, **in some circumstances,** the same thing. We should have said no to the conservatives, who hate regulation, and are constantly trying to undo it, because it hinders unrestrained capitalism. We just witnessed what lack of restraint can accomplish. We should have demanded that regulators actually enforce the regulations that exist. We should demand **more** regulations (not less) that protect us from the stupid, and the sometimes-predatory portions of our society.

When will this recession be over?

It won't (any job growth that we will see will be at the lower end; you know, hamburger flippers, Wal-Mart greeters, part time jobs, etc.). At least it won't until we force our political leaders to make some drastic and fundamental changes to a large part of the way we are currently doing business. You've seen some examples in this post, and will see many more examples in successive posts. Until we face up to the need to restrain all the idiots (both greedy and do-gooder), this economy will continue to be stagnant.

Here we go again!

The purpose of our government (and the people who are employed by our government) can be summed up by a sign, which I saw on a police car in California, *"To protect, and to serve".* To that, I would like to add one word *"-everyone".* Not just the rich at the expense of   the poor, or the poor at the expense of the rich, not the powerful at the expense of the weak, or vice-versa. Our government exists ***"To protect, and to serve - everyone".*** And if that means compromise—so be it.

Chapter 10

Wall Street Reform

Starting when George W. Bush ran for his first term as President, the conservatives, with George leading the way, were pushing to end Social Security in order to have it replaced by private IRA-type investment accounts. Supposedly, this was to allow the bulk of the citizenry to be able to have more money to retire on than they would have with the Social Security program. This sounds great. However, when you look at it more closely, it starts to smell like yesterdays fish. What it was--was another desire by the rich, the investment banks, and brokerages etc., to get their hands on a vast pool of money that it currently does not have access to. This money would be placed into a game where the majority of Americans neither understand the rules, nor have any chance of prospering because the game is rigged against nearly all those who don't play it full time (and with very large amounts of money) as their vocation.

I know this sounds like some kind of anti-capitalist rant, but nothing could be farther from the truth. I really am not a communist. It is a rant to level the playing field for all and make it safer for the average investor to play the game--

because the stock market is a game that is, indeed, rigged.

Let's take my own case as an example. By the time I retire, I-- and the companies that I have worked for will have paid (in my name) into Social Security over $172,000. At the time that I retire I will be able to receive a little over $2000 per month. Unfortunately, the funds to pay it will come from the taxpayers who are still working. The conservatives are correct in pointing out that it is one gigantic "Ponzie" scheme. And every one knows that all "Ponzie" schemes eventually collapse because they depend on an infinitely expanding pool of investors (an impossibility). However, if the money had been instead invested in Series E savings bonds at an average of just 4% I would have a next egg of $491,000. That is quite enough for me to live off of the rest of my life quite comfortably. Especially since (except for the most recent stock market collapse) in most years I was averaging more than a 20% return (and now--even more). But here is the kicker. I understand much (but not all) of how this game is played (I'm still learning), and yet I still frequently have my bloody head handed to me. There is too much uncertainty and corruption in the market place to expect those people who are woefully ignorant of how to play the game to entrust their retirements to those people and institutions whose goal is to separate them from their money. A good way to wean us off of the Social Security teat might be to phase in (like in my example) using government bonds, or (better yet) TIPS (Treasury Inflation Protected Securities), to be delivered or rationed out at the time of retirement. This will give the retirees enough time to learn the game if they wish to. But the one key element necessary to make that game work is Wall Street reform. That is, we have to change the rules to make it much harder to be ripped off. Then the government must oversee and vigorously enforce the rules. This would allow all but the most problematic of our society to get off of Social Security while simultaneously improving our retirement and reducing the social security tax burden.

See? I'm not a communist. I want to be able to make more money and pay less tax, the same as most people. It is just that I don't want to either economically harm anyone else, or allow others to be harmed. I also want to aid those who truly need it. The problem with Capitalism is not that it is a corrupt system. Capitalism is an amoral system. That is, it is a system devoid of morality, or immorality. It takes on the morality of the people using it. A quote by Lenin comes to mind. When asked to define a capitalist, Lenin said, ***"A capitalist is someone who will sell you the rope that you are going to hang him with"***. Think about that for a minute. Another view can be understood by the phrase "Questus Gratia Questus" (profit for the sake of profit). Both of these phrases illustrate that the people whose goal is to enrich themselves at the immediate or future expense to others (and sometimes themselves) are at the heart of what makes the system appear to be immoral and corrupt.

In the previous Blog posting I had talked about what, and who, caused the latest economic calamity. Now I will talk about just a few of the things that need to be done to make the markets a relatively safe place to invest for our future.

Commodity futures caused a totally unwarranted run up in prices, which, if left unchecked, would have eventually brought the world economy to its knees even without the bursting of the housing bubble. It still has the capacity to ruin our economy yet. The solution is:

1. Eliminate the stock exchange traded securities that deal in commodities. These have become an asset class rather than a perishable class. Most investors do not trade asset class investments frequently. The long term holding of futures contracts, without regard to the short-term fundamentals affecting supply and demand--grossly distorts the supply or demand, which causes unrealistic prices in the market. If someone wants to invest in commodities, they could still go to the commodity markets, do their due diligence, and take their chances.

Here are some other problems/solutions.

2. End Short-selling--totally. Probably the biggest problem in the stock market is the allowing of "short-selling". The

proponents of this corrupt practice **always claim** that short selling benefits the market by contributing to the liquidity of the market. Most people hear that, and assume that it is the truth because someone that sounds like they are someone who really knows what they are talking about said it, and it sounded reasonable. They do (if they really are an expert) know what they are talking about. It is just that person is lying through his teeth. Short-selling only **artificially** increases the liquidity on the supply side, thus, **artificially** driving the price of the stock (being sold-short) lower. To illustrate, lets say that at an instant in time there are people bidding to buy 100,000 shares of a company for $10. At that same instant there are only people willing to sell 5,000 shares of that company at that price. The law of supply and demand dictates that if the price the buyers are willing to pay goes up, more sellers will be willing to sell. The resulting price (maybe $10.75) is the result of supply meeting demand. Short-selling is the selling of a stock that you do not have, but have borrowed from someone else (for a small fee), and must be replaced at some time in the future, ideally at a much lower price. That is where the short-seller makes the profit.

Instead of buy low and sell high (as we've all been taught), short sellers first sell high and then buy low. Both instances buy low and sell high, but the order is opposite. Now, in that same scenario above, if you offer 100,000 short-shares for sale on top of the 5,000 legitimate shares for sale, you now have an artificially created imbalance on the supply side that will result in a price of maybe $9.75. The "big buck" guys and hedge funds use this tactic, and by piling on when they see that a stock is being picked on (called a Bear-raid) they can continue to drive the price lower and lower before they must purchase the replacement shares that they borrowed to start this process. In their perfect scenario they would drive a stock to an extremely low price. When that happens, a company can no longer raise funds by selling stock, and may ultimately collapse. This results in the borrowed stock that was sold at $9.75 being covered by purchasing shares at a price that approaches $0. It is then a (both a figurative and a literal) killing in the market. Another variation of this is when an investment bank loans a company a great deal of money. A condition of the loan is that the loan can be converted to stock, at the banks discretion, instead of being paid back in cash. A second condition is that the company must "loan" a very large number of shares to the bank so that the bank may "hedge" their risk. What then happens is that the bank then short-sells those loaned shares, artificially driving the share price lower. If they do it right, they can then drive the price so low that they can then own an artificially large portion of the company, which they then sell at a much higher price later after they stop "shorting" the stock and allow it's price to rise to it's proper level. Or they can also **not** short it themselves, but loan it out to short-sellers and collect interest while the short-sellers do the dirty work, and as a result make even more money. Large funds loan their shares to shorter-sellers to increase their income while at the same time allowing the short-sellers to create the short term market volatility that they profit by). I have seen the interest rates for some shorted stocks as high as 34%. You will hear experts talk about the need for "hedging" a lot. You can hedge your investment by using "put" options. "Put" options can protect your investment and, at the same time, not distort the market. Short selling is a corrupt practice that is used to distort the supply and demand balance and manipulate prices, and is intended to enrich while, at the same time, economically harming virtually everyone else not shorted. Put Options are a bet that the price will go down, and if it does--you make money. Short selling makes profit by the **destruction of other people's value**. I can't stress this enough--**it's corrupt**.

A daily loan can allow eight to ten shorts to borrow the same shares, thus resetting the SHO-fail-to-deliver clock each time, which makes all of these counterfeit stocks appear to be legitimate shares. The broker-dealers have an incentive to do this activity because they charge each short-seller for lent stock as well as the transaction fees.

An **illegal practice** that is condoned by many Brokers is the **"naked short sale".** That is selling a stock short without first borrowing it. Occasionally there have been more shares of a stock sold than there was--total shares in existence.

Both of these practices can be seen in this next example.

A classic example of this involved Global Links Corporation. How did the wholesale counterfeiting of shares decimate a company's stock price? Global Links is a company that provided computer services to the real estate industry. By early 2005, their stock price had dropped to a fraction of a cent. At that point, an investor, Robert Simpson, **purchased 100% of Global Links stock (1,158,064) issued and outstanding shares.** He immediately took delivery of his shares, filed the appropriate forms with the SEC, and disclosed **he owned all of the company's stock**. His total investment was $5,205. The share price was $.00434. **The day after** he acquired **all** of the company's shares the volume on the over-the-counter market was 37 million shares. The following day he saw 22 million shares change hands. Simpson did not trade a single share. Think about that, people. **One man owned all the stock,** which was a little over 1.1 million shares, and **didn't sell one single share**, yet over the next two days approximately 59 million shares changed hands. This clearly means there were invisible counterfeit shares created out of thin air through naked short selling by individuals, brokers or market makers.

One more thing will illustrate the corruption of "short-selling". As I already mentioned--legitimate short selling requires the borrowing of the stock that you wish to sell-short. You must pay a fee (interest) to the holder of the stock for each share that you wish to borrow. Your Broker (who is supposed to be working for you) makes a commission on your purchase, then is making a commission from loaning your stock to someone who will drive-down the price of that stock, and indeed, then also makes another commission on the "short sale" as well. Wait! The Broker isn't done yet. He then makes yet another commission when the short seller must purchase the stock to cover his position. He also may make another commission off you, if you got scared by the price drop and sold your shares. And if you have a margin account with the broker, he can loan your stock without your permission and doesn't even have to give you the interest for the loan of your stock.

Some Broker-Dealers have also been known to change cash accounts to margin accounts without telling the owner the real motive behind the move, or take shares from IRA accounts or take shares from cash accounts, and lend restricted shares. Pretty neat scam, huh? No wonder these crooks keep spouting their BS about bringing needed liquidity to the market.

3. Eliminate leveraged and ultra-leveraged exchange-traded funds.

These are exchange-traded funds that return two and three times the daily market movement, both up and down, of the stocks held in the fund. For every Long fund there is a corresponding Short Fund, that is, funds that are only short seller funds (I already pointed out the damage that short-selling does to the market). The shills tout that the advantage of the exchange-traded funds is the inherent diversity, which really appeals to the "couch potato" investor (which most of us are). The problem is that these funds are traded as stocks, and not like funds. When you buy or sell a Mutual Fund you must wait until the market closes for the day before you find out what you made, or lost, for the Mutual Fund shares. Since exchange-traded funds are traded as if they were a stock, and because of the violent price swings of the leveraged funds, they have become a favorite playground for day-traders. That results in a pendulum effect of price movement, and extreme price volatility, but with little overall appreciation. Ideally, we should get rid of exchange-traded funds altogether, but an improvement would be had if we ended the leveraged and ultra-funds, and also made fund value settlement at the end of the day (like with mutual funds). It is not a coincidence that the market became lousy shortly after exchange-traded funds became popular, and short selling and day trading became prevalent.

Short selling is at the heart of nearly all of the bad things that happen, on a daily basis, in the stock market.

4. Treat "Credit Default Swaps" as what they are--Insurance. As you saw in my earlier posting how AIG nearly brought the

economy to its knees because of all the "derivatives" that they and their trading partners created and traded. Many of these "derivatives" in a normal economy serve little or no purpose except to provide an avenue for traders to make money on by trading them. However, when things go bad, they have the ability to make things much worse. The derivative that I'm talking about here is the credit default swaps. A credit default swap is basically an insurance policy that pays if a credit obligation is defaulted on. The difference is that it is in force for the duration of the obligation, regardless how many times it is traded, and pays off to whoever possesses the swap, and not necessarily to whoever holds the covered obligation. It should be that it pays only the owner of the insured property--like any insurance policy. I heard the head of one of the investment banks say that we shouldn't restrict or regulate these things, because if we do stop it--the investors will just invest their money in countries that allow it. Again, a shortsighted view in the interest of short term profits. If another country wants to act stupid and go broke, let them. Our government already has agencies and rules in place; now we just need to fine tune the rules and lay the hammer to anyone who breaks them. Stop turning a blind eye to the perpetrators.

5. Scrap the rating agency's, and create a single non-profit organization. Having for-profit companies (agencies) compete for the business of the banks leads to dishonest ratings for the

products the banks want to sell. It is a conflict of interest. If they don't give a Banks product a good rating, the bank may not give it any future business.

6. Set a reasonable debt to asset ratio and then enforce it. You remember that part of the reason that the banks got in so much trouble was that not only the government allowed them to increase the debt to asset ratio from 11:1 to 13:1, but then looked the other way when the banks exceeded that new maximum by 400-500%. Also the real values of some assets were not considered when assigning values to the mortgage bundles. The government needs to watch these institutions closer because many of them will always be inclined to cheat if they think that they can get by with it. After all, it's only against the law if you get caught, right? They also must be required to assign a realistic value to those mortgage bundles as well as any other asset whose value currently is determined by active trading. Neither pie in the sky valuations that the banks want, nor the volatile trading valuations that imply an unrealistic value are a good idea.

7. As long as I am on a roll, how about ending computerized trading (also known as High Frequency Trading)? Think--short selling--on steroids. Have you heard of the market "flash-crashes" of the last few years? Automated trading caused them. And automated trading also accelerates the gigantic "Bear-raids" on individual stocks.

8. If we won't end the horrible practices of Automated trading and Day-trading then lets at least put a two or three cents per share transaction tax on each and every trade for both practices, and enforce the uptick rule that is already on the books (but—unfortunately--is also ignored). Or--here's a thought; require **every** share of stock be held for at least 24 hours before it can be sold. None of that would hurt the average investor, but with tens of millions of shares being traded back and forth, thousands of times a minute, it can be a big financial roadblock for these Bozo's (Hedge Funds, High Frequency Traders, and Day traders) who are killing us with their greed and manipulation.

9. Require **all trades** to be accomplished by Brokers and made public--on the exchanges--as they are made, and **eliminate** pre-market and after-hours trading. Zero--Zip--Nada--None!!! That would truly be free-market and supply-and-demand based pricing. Currently the big short-sellers make their multiple small-lot purchases (to cover) during the day, but report them in bulk after hours so as to not push the price up while they are buying. The really big traders make their trades privately off-line (Dark Pool). By doing this they are again distorting the demand side of the equation to their advantage.

10. End Market Maker exemptions and advantages. From Wikipedia· *In the United States, the New York Sock*

Exchange (NYSE) and American Stock Exchange (AMEX), among others, have Designated Market Makers, formerly known as "specialists", who act as the official market maker for a given security. The market makers provide a required amount of liquidity to the security's market, and take the other side of trades when there are short-term buy-and-sell-side imbalances in customer orders. **In return, the specialist is granted various informational and trade execution advantages.**

Other U.S. exchanges, most prominently the NASDAQ Stock Exchange, employ several competing official market makers in a security. These market makers are required to maintain two-sided markets during exchange hours and are obligated to buy and sell at their displayed bids and offers. They typically do not receive the trading advantages a specialist does, but they do get some, such as the **ability to naked short a stock,** *i.e., selling it without borrowing it. In most situations, only official market makers are permitted to engage in naked shorting.* **As of October 2008 there were over two thousand market makers in the USA** *and over a hundred in Canada.*

These are exemptions and advantages that are given to some stock market whales (killer?) legally exempting them from timely reporting transactions and the naked shorting rules. Notice the "liquidity" excuse again. This is just good sounding double-talk to get those who don't understand to go along with their manipulative BS. Also, Market Maker exemptions can be temporarily acquired (rented) from the official Market Makers by devious processes such as Reverse Conversions. So those two thousand market makers in the USA can really amount to many tens of thousands of mischief-makers creating havoc with the markets at any one time.

By putting, and enforcing boundaries on Wall Street, we can make it easier for nearly all of us to enjoy a better, more **affluent** and **secure** future. It won't satisfy the avarice of the Gordon Gecko group of "Greed is good" disciples. But those people will still be able to make lots of dough; it is just that they will have to do so without intentionally harming others. We need to **shame our political leaders** into curbing the excesses of the avaricious predators influencing our futures.

Here we go again.

The purpose of our government (and the people who are employed by our government) can be summed up by a sign, which I saw on a police car in California, *"To protect, and to serve"*. To that, I would like to add one word *"-EVERYONE"*. Not just the rich at the expense of the poor, or the poor at the expense of the rich, not the powerful at the expense of the weak, or vice-versa. Our government exists *"TO PROTECT AND TO SERVE - EVERYONE"*. And if that means compromise—so be it.

Chapter 11

Healthcare Reform

(This was posted while Obama-care was being debated in 2010, but the observations are still valid.)

I was going to wait awhile until the smoke clears to get into this subject, but everyone out there is going NUTS right now. I wanted to wait and find out what this brand new bill contains, but the lack of accurate information isn't holding our political leaders back from both throwing out misinformation and from inciting the more radical of their constituents to threats of violence.

OK everybody, take a deep breath and calm down (again).

No bill ever goes unchanged. The political process that we employ requires all kinds of smelly inclusions in order to get enough votes to pass. What then happens is that congress goes back and readdresses most of those onerous items, and gets rid of them over time. It is easy to get a majority in congress to eliminate any individual facet of a bill that is bad, but which was only included in the original bill because that was what was required to get a particular representative to vote for the over-all bill; think "the Nebraska Kickback" and "the

Louisiana-Purchase" (no--not the original Louisiana Purchase).

As for those idiot Sates Attorney Generals that are going to challenge the Constitutionality of requiring mandatory insurance coverage; that's pretty disingenuous--when just about every state requires mandatory auto liability insurance coverage (not unconstitutional?). Oh, yeah, I forgot. Auto liability insurance suppliers make political donations and payoffs. A government run insurance program doesn't line their pockets. I'll bet if we offered our representatives a way for them to profit--they would all line up behind the bill's passage and think of ways to wax poetic about its virtues and the need to increase its scope.

Pretty much everybody acknowledges the need for health-care reform. Well, not really everybody. The "wealthy" are made up of two different groups. There are the wealthy people who have a conscience, appreciate their fortune, and don't mind helping those less fortunate than themselves while still remaining wealthy. There is also a group of wealthy people, who are disciples of Darwin; survival of the fittest; I got mine--get your own. These people only pay lip service to the concept of "win-win". Some are open about it, but most of that group secretly desire "win-lose". After all, what's the point of winning if someone doesn't lose? These people can be charitable, but mostly to stuff that gets them on the society pages in the paper. You know--a new wing to an arts center or hospital, or a scholarship fund, etc. It is just the kind of stuff that gets your name engraved on a building, addition, or plaque, and your picture in the paper identifying you as a generous philanthropist. They usually don't give near as much, if anything, that goes to a free clinic, charitable hospital, homeless shelter, or soup kitchen. You know, the kinds of gifts that actually help the less fortunate. Unfortunately, it's this last group of "the wealthy" that provides the funds for the ultra-conservatives to get elected, and stay elected. Let's look rationally at some of the opposition to this healthcare reform bill.

First, there is the "health-care will be limited, or rationed" argument. There is absolutely nothing in any proposals that I have heard, or read, that even hints at this. This bill is about being just another insurance OPTION that would (hopefully) be available at a more affordable price to more people. Insurance plans do not limit anything but what they will pay for specific procedures and overall costs. This (being an insurance plan, like Medicare) is no different. If you want better insurance there is nothing to prevent you from purchasing it. Additionally--just watch--there may eventually be a plethora (I've been wanting to find an excuse to use that word for a long time) of supplemental plans for sale, just as with Medicare.

The second argument is that it will restrict our doctor-choice. Again, this is an insurance plan. All doctors do not accept all insurance plans for payment. Think Medicare; every doctor does not accept Medicare, but many do. And you can always buy something else that a particular doctor does accept, or go to a different doctor.

Thirdly, we hear the shrill voices say, *"It's going to cost too much."* Let's look at that for a moment. What this plan is intended to do is provide lower cost health-care to the group of people who inundate the emergency rooms of hospitals at great expense to the public.

These people do not have insurance to cover normal visits, so they either go to the emergency room for trivial things, or they let it go until they are in really bad shape. Either way it costs a lot more than if they had affordable insurance. These hospitals get their funds from the government, and from charities. They also raise the prices for their services to everyone else, to cover the shortfalls. So, we are going to basically replace very expensive health-care for those people, with less expensive health-care. In both cases, the rest of us are already paying for it, but the difference is that we will all be paying a lower cost for it directly through taxes, instead of a through a higher cost divided between current taxes, increased rates, and charities.

The fourth argument is "the naked power grab by the Democrats".

Please! Any power grab there--is available for the taking **by either party**. It's just that the constituency that benefits the most (believe it or not, everyone will benefit to some degree) is not the constituency that lines the conservative Republicans pockets.

There are a lot of people out there who can't buy insurance at any price, or if they can, it is more than they can afford.

Take me for instance. I am over sixty, overweight, diabetic, suffered congestive heart failure, have severe osteoarthritis in both knees and hips, and can't get insurance **at any price**! For those of you who just saw that, and said to yourself *"No wonder this a**h*** is for this bill, he's looking for a handout"*, I am getting very good care by the VA, and will be getting Medicare in a couple of years. This bill will very likely have no effect on me.

My mention of the V.A. provides an opportune segue into my last thought.

I feel that this bill does not go far enough. Hold on! Calm down! Hear me out!

I feel that the government should approach health-care with a two-prong approach like they do for education. That is, both a public and a private option. I know, many areas have really bad public education systems, but that is because, as I've mentioned before, funding is provided by local property taxes.

Low property values are synonymous with low property taxes, and we all know that you get exactly what you pay for.

What most people do not know is that when comparing the same services between the VA, and Medicare, the VA provides those same services for 80% of the cost to Medicare.

It is easy to see why when you look at both as business models.

Cost centers for VA:

1. VA Infrastructure

2. VA Accounting

3. VA Staff

4. VA Cost Centers **(no profit)**

Cost centers for Medicare:

1. Hospital Infrastructure

2. Hospital Accounting

3. Hospital Staff

4. Hospital liability insurance

5. Hospital **Profit** at each cost center

6. Medicare Infrastructure

7. Medicare Accounting

8. Medicare Staff

9. Fraud by providers

As you can see, the cost model for Medicare Insurance versus the direct health care provided by the VA cannot help but be higher. Each of those cost centers is a hand out saying, "give me".

Now look at the normal private insurance cost structure.

1. Hospital Infrastructure

2. Hospital Accounting

3. Hospital Staff

4. Hospital liability insurance

5. Hospital Profit

6. Insurance Co. Infrastructure

7. Insurance Co. Staff

8. Insurance Co. Accounting

9. Insurance Co. Profit

10. Insurance Co. Legal department

11. Fraud by providers

As you can see, the cost model for private insurance is much higher than either VA or Medicare because of Insurance Co. Profit, and Legal Department.

My first choice for health-care reform is for a government run parallel heath system similar to that of education, and that is-- both private--and public. That way if the medical care is performed directly by the government, there is much less opportunity for fraud and over or double billing (only possible with insurance) by providers. As illustrated previously by the VA example, this is also the cheapest way to provide healthcare.

My second choice is to extend Medicare to everyone. However, Medicare should be reformed. We should take a look at what someone can receive with Medicare. I, for one, do not like to help pay for some clowns need for Viagra, or for a power chair for someone when a cane, crutches, or manual wheelchair will suffice. I would qualify for a power chair (even though I don't really need one) under Medicare.

We should also really hammer the hell out of anyone caught defrauding Medicare. Offer a sizable reward/bounty for people to turn in cheats or fraud perpetrators.

My third choice is the way this bill came out. It doesn't do much, except put some very weak reins on the insurance companies (an improvement), and force the poor (who can't afford to pay for insurance) to pay for insurance. As I've said before--they're called "the poor" for a very good reason.

Because medical liability insurance is too large a piece of the cost pie, tort reform is absolutely essential, and would greatly reduce costs for everyone but the VA. It should be, but won't be, one of the fixes to the current bill. Don't hold your breath. Most of our political representatives are lawyers, and they are not about to reform the cash cow milked by their attorney brothers. If the government were to expand Medicare or, better yet, VA type care to everyone, we should make it the law that if you accept government sponsored medical care you cannot sue. Period! Doctors and medical workers could still be fired, or lose their licenses, but they and the hospitals would not need to have liability insurance, thus eliminating a very large part of the public run healthcare costs in one fell-swoop.

There are plenty of really bad hospitals and hospital systems out there. These hospitals could be purchased by the govt. and run by, or like, the VA (the VA actually does very good work over all. They saved my life. The crap you hear about the VA is from intellectually dishonest people with their own axes to grind). This would not eliminate private hospitals or insurance companies. Those would still exist as an option just as private schools co-exist with the public school systems. They would just be motivated to provide superior service at a somewhat more competitive price.

I recently was visiting with a lady who was railing about "Obama-care". She spouted all the usual stuff (see above). I then went over the same stuff that I just bored you with here. She then countered with, *"But I shouldn't have to pay for someone else."*

I said, *"You're right, I don't want to pay for them either, so we should just say, about a person that can't afford help, the hell with him--he's poor-- let him die."* She paused, with a pained look on her face, and said, *"No, that's not what I mean."*

Then she pointed out, that it's not right that we should pay for the benefit of people who could afford insurance, but are gaming the system. I said, *"You're right, we should let some poor honest sucker die because there will be some cheats."* Again, *"No, that's not what I mean"*. Then she played her trump card. *"It will be impossible for the government to enforce it."* I said, *"You're right again, let the poor S.O.B. die because the government can't enforce everyone's participation."* She then admitted that--that's not so good either.

Folks, this bill is a start. I personally don't feel that it goes far enough, but the health-care of 2030 won't resemble the bill of 2010. We will change some   of   what   is   needed, compromise where necessary, and eventually be closer to where we need to be. And guess what--the **overall** cost of health-care will be less than it is now; taxes will be higher, but you probably will have much less premiums (if any) to pay as an offset. Why do you think the insurance companies are fighting so hard against this? As with anything else, when you want to discover someone's motivation, **follow the money**. Anything that we do to improve health-care for everyone--also reduces the vast (my own hyperbole) profits the insurance companies, providers, and lawyers are now making.

Insurance, as it was invented by the Chinese many centuries ago, was intended as a way to spread the risk (and cost) for the benefit of everyone. The way it is implemented now, is that it does not spread the risk, but instead segments the risk. By segmenting the risk it drives out the people who would actually need it, leaving the insurance companies collecting beau coup premiums and paying out next to nothing.

Some of you are now thinking, *" I thought that this clown was a moderate. But this crap is liberal, or even communistic."* As I said in my fist post, moderates tend to have thought out, reasoned, individual positions that can be liberal, or conservative, and anywhere in between. Just wait! When I get on security, defense, and immigration, some of you are going to think that I'm some kind of a Neo-Nazi. Then again, I am also decidedly slightly liberal when it comes to civil liberties.

But I promise, I am not bi-polar.

The only thing that the words health and wealth should have in common is that they rhyme.

The purpose of our government (and the people who are employed by our government) can be summed up by a sign, which I saw on a police car in California, *"To protect, and to serve".* To that, I would like to add one word *" –everyone".* Not just the rich at the expense of the poor, or the poor at the expense of the rich, not the powerful at the expense of the weak, or vice-versa. Our government exists ***"To protect, and to serve –everyone".*** And if that means compromise-- so be it.

Chapter 12

Let's Overhaul Welfare

I don't want to get rid of "welfare"; I just want to make it more equitable (there's my favorite word again) and inclusive.

When I was a child in Nebraska our family rented a farm that had been known locally as the "Poor-Farm". It seems that, some generations previously, it was a place where people that were homeless or penniless had been sent for food and shelter in exchange for work on the farm.

Later, when we moved into the town of Fremont, Nebraska I saw that there were WWII Quonset huts (like on 'Gomer Pyle, USMC') that were occupied by poor families.

Now the government pays rent (section eight) for high quality houses in the suburbs so that the poor people won't have to endure the stigma of welfare housing. In many cases this housing is better than their neighbors (who work and struggle with a mortgage) can afford. Fair? No way! Taint equitable neither. [Note to editor: I know that isn't grammatically correct. Leave it; it's intentional.]

Instead of welfare families getting a healthy and nutritious variety of foods, they are given food stamps (now debit cards, because, again, they shouldn't have to endure any stigma) and end up buying Twinkies, potato chips, soda-pop, and candy bars; or even selling their benefits for discounted cash so that they then can buy booze, drugs, or cigarettes. Disgusting abuse of our public largess.

I have no problem providing **basic** shelter, good healthcare, and nutritious food. The problem I have is "giving away the farm" to these people.

They **should** be housed in free or low-cost shelter. They **should** get food from a "welfare store" where they would be issued their weekly allotment of approved nutritious food. They **should** be required (if able) to work at some kind of public service in return. There **should** be a stigma attached to their living off the public. No one will look down on the truly unfortunate, but there must be some incentives for them to eventually, if possible, take care of themselves.

When we lived in Fremont, there was an orphanage located there that was run by the Masons. I had a couple of classmates who lived there who were well cared for and well adjusted, and also didn't seem to have any real complaints. Of course, we were only about 30 miles away from Boys Town (our high school played them in basketball and football), so orphanages were a common experience that we thought nothing about. Our only problem with Boys Town was that they were always beating us in sports. Where are the orphanages today? The government now pays people a great deal of money for each child to be foster parents. So much so, that, in our East Texas area, "foster-children" is synonymous with "cash-crop". I know of one couple (junkies and drunks that have no jobs, and no desire to get any) that has four foster children. They live in the squalor of a **small** travel-trailer with no toilet or showers, or even running water; for that, they must use the park facilities. They do, however, have plenty of beer and weed. The children were stealing to get by. An orphanage has got to be better, and, in the long run, cheaper, as well as less degrading than that.

Now**, what about corporate welfare?**

We should stop giving grants, government backed "low-cost" loans, and subsidies and tax breaks of any kind, to any and all companies, including farmers, and also stop giving hand-outs from states and cities to encourage businesses to relocate there or to encourage their current resident businesses to forgo leaving. No one benefits from that practice. Not the states and cities who lose the company, because they also lose the employment, and the tax revenue. And certainly not the states and cities that gain the company, because they forego any tax revenue, and frequently give the company grants to cover the cost of training. The only people who gain are the fat cats running this win-lose zero-sum scam.

A favorite whipping boy, "Big Oil", comes to mind. The government hands out enormous subsidies to the oil companies. And who are the companies that are some of the most profitable companies on the planet? Oil companies! Not only are they accepting our largess, but also, in many cases, they are working against our own interests. Our companies take our money and then try to find ways to not pay it back. In addition, they also try to pay less tax while, they are at the same time, paying their management teams hundreds of millions of dollars in salaries and bonuses for doing it. Yeah! They receive bonuses for succeeding in getting their companies on welfare, regardless of whether they need it or not.

All our corporate leaders speak out of both sides of their mouths. Out of the one side they talk about wanting to have a "free market", and at the same time out of the other side they cry-poor and have their hand out wanting free / cheap money from us without regard as to whether they are profitable or not. It is one thing to provide **critical and temporary** help to emerging or strategic industries, but it is incredibly stupid to give money to well established and profitable enterprises. On the other hand, it sure is profitable for our representatives who get political contributions, perks, votes and outright bribes from the recipients of our government largess.

It's the same with sovereign welfare. That's just another name for foreign aid.

We should end **all** foreign aid (in all forms). It is almost impossible to get accurate figures on how much this country hands out each year, and a lot of aid gets classified as something else. After 2007 some aid is no longer required to be reported. Foreign Aid is just throwing money down a rat-hole.

We are showering cash and goods on all kinds of countries that frequently work against us, and many of them intend to do us harm.

Giving cash and goods to third-world countries, though well intentioned, rarely affects the population that it is intended to help; it only enriches their corrupt leaders, or makes the recipient country complacent and comfortable with the way things are. Hmmm, kinda like our Congress.

We give money to Pakistan, who harbors terrorists bent on our destruction. We give aid to N. Korea in return for halting their nuclear ambitions. They accept our aid, and then continue building nukes. We give aid to Russia, who then tries to thwart us at every turn on the world stage because of their jealousy. We have been giving continuous aid to Israel since their founding, and they thanked us by (unless I remember wrongly) sinking one of our boats a couple of decades ago. We give aid to rebels of bad countries so that they can overthrow their bad leaders. The problem arises when, after winning, they are just as bad as the people that were overthrown. Iraq and Afghanistan are good examples of that, as well as Cuba. We offer our treasure and blood to countries that turn on us the first chance they get.

Our attitude should be **"to hell with them all, they can sink or swim. And if they want to screw with us, or do us harm, we can help them sink faster"**. We have to take care of ourselves.

If we were to stop giving aid to corporations and countries, and redo the way we treat welfare, we would probably have enough money to take very good care of our own people here.

Oh, oh, Here it comes.

The purpose of our government (and the people who are employed by our government) can be summed up by a sign, which I saw on a police car in California, *"To protect, and to serve"*. To that, I would like to add one word *" –everyone"*. Not just the rich at the expense of the poor, or the poor at the expense of the rich, not the powerful at the expense of the weak, or vice-versa. Our government exists ***"To protect, and to serve - everyone"***. And if that means compromise-- so be it.

Chapter 13

Immigration Reform

I haven't checked out the details of the latest brouhaha over the illegal alien crackdown in Arizona, but there is no need. The details may change, but the opposing sides and their rationale remain constant.

The liberal left, when absent any cogent logic for their position of allowing nearly unlimited immigration, accuse anybody who wants to staunch the flow of illegal aliens of using racial profiling and discrimination. And that is their main illogical weapon also regarding the war against terror and the struggle against drug trafficking. They also have an uneasy partnership with a group who is neither uniquely left nor right. The people of this group are those who want to flood the labor markets with cheap labor--so that they can drive labor costs down and thus reap greater profits. The Democratic Party also supports them because unlimited immigration from south of the border means perceived massive increases in Democratic Party membership and voters because the Democratic Party is perceived to be the Party of the less fortunate and downtrodden.

The right wants to close the borders to illegal aliens for two reasons. The first is to make it harder for terrorists and drug traffickers to gain access to this country, and the second is to stop the flood of illegal aliens into this country, which is (in no small way) partly responsible for the decline in both the size, affluence, and influence of the middle class. I don't blame the illegal aliens for wanting to be here, and I don't blame their relatives for wanting to bring them here. But I am, however, eliminating them from the decision process with regard to this issue simply because their position is totally biased (understandably so) for unlimited immigration without regard to the harm it does to this country. I am also not going to discuss the Democratic Party's willingness to cripple the future economic security of this country in order to get an increase in near term Democratic voters, because this position is so disgusting and obvious to anyone that isn't blinded by party loyalty that it doesn't need my discussing it further. Regarding closing off our borders and booting the illegal aliens out, I side with the conservatives (at least the conservatives who are not trying to profit from the importation of cheap labor). No kidding! Finally! I'm not hammering the conservatives.

The problem with the true liberals is that they do not take a position based on a well thought out examination of facts, followed by a reasoned decision. They come to all their positions as a result of knee-jerk reactions to any perceived injustice, and a feeling that everyone is basically good and fair, and will prove it if they can only be given a chance. Riiight! Kum-Ba-Yah! Why can't we all just get along? It's all based on feelings and emotions--with absolutely no reasoned thought. Whoa, that sounds like Bill O'Reilly. Sorry about that, but he would be right.

The liberals do not want extra scrutiny placed on young middle-eastern Muslim men traveling to this country, or Latino's traveling in this country. It's racial profiling; and that, as we all know, is just so wrong.

That is just such a great big load of BS!!!

If a significant number of terrorists had been young, good-looking, blonde, Swedish Hindu women (I have no idea if there ever are any Hindu's, or is it Hindi, in Sweden) we should be giving **them** extra scrutiny at airports. In fact, I would volunteer to work at security in any airport just to give them some extra up close and personal scrutiny. However, it is a fact that nearly all of the terrorists are young middle-eastern men of the Islamic religion. Damn straight--young middle-eastern men of the Islamic faith SHOULD be targeted and scrutinized. To do less SHOULD be considered criminally negligent by anyone with an IQ greater than that God gave a gnat. If terrorists start to appear in significant numbers from other demographics, then we SHOULD profile those categories as well.

Obviously we are unfairly picking on our Latin neighbors by the increased efforts there at border security for both terrorist security and for the security of our economy while ignoring our Canadian border. Profiling? As Sarah Palin would say, ***"You Betcha!"*** Last I heard we don't have tens of millions of Canadians streaming across our border to flood the labor market with cheap labor. It's coming from Mexico! And we need to stop it now! It is killing the economy of this country.

It is all about our security, which is, at the same time both "Terrorist" security and "Economic" security. I'm not going to get into the issue of why we need to keep terrorists from entering our country. That's all too obvious. I am, however, going to go over the lack of economic security that is causing what is soon going to be irreparable damage. That is the artificial flooding of the labor markets with cheap labor, and also the resulting siphoning of treasure out of this country.

The worst group that supports such unlimited immigration is made up of unprincipled people of every political leaning who are only interested in cheap labor so as to make more profit. They mostly want unlimited immigration so that they can keep labor prices down. If they can't get unlimited immigration then they want at least greatly increased legal immigration. If they can't get that, they then push for lax enforcement of our immigration laws.

Forty years ago, you could make a good middle class living by working in meat packing plants, or working in construction. Not now. Wages have been stagnant in those industries for the last thirty years or more because the packing companies and construction companies have gradually replaced our own citizen workers with cheap illegal immigrants.

[Added in 2013—I just saw on the evening news that out of 600,000 construction workers in Texas alone—400,000 are illegal aliens. That is 400,000 jobs that would go to our own citizens, and they would be at a higher wage because the labor supply would no longer be artificially rigged. Those higher paying jobs would, indeed, increase the construction costs, but because there would now be 400,000 people earning a living wage (thus being able to afford spending money into the economy instead of taking money out of the economy) the economy would increase. With an increasing economy we would very easily be able to afford the increased construction costs. Those 400,000 illegal workers spend minimally here while the bulk of their earnings go to their families in their native countries. They also are a drag on our welfare systems.]

After the collapse of the Soviet Union the heads of the Schneider National and J. B. Hunt trucking companies lobbied congress trying to get them to allow the trucking companies to bring in tens of thousands of truck drivers from the former Soviet Bloc countries. They were hoping to be able to exploit cheap foreign labor like the meat packing industry and construction industry has, and get some of the same labor cost benefits as all the manufacturing industries that closed up shop here, and moved first to Mexico and then to Asia.

Fortunately for us, Congress grew some cajone's, put their collective foot down, and said no. So there is still one group that can still make a decent wage (Trucking). However, it is still in danger because of the ongoing efforts to allow Mexican trucks and drivers to operate, with little limits, in this country. If allowed free hand in this country the Mexican driven trucks will get more and more freight, edging out our own people because of the reduced freight costs due to cheap Mexican drivers.

Another negative aspect of our current lack of immigration enforcement is the massive outflow of currency to our neighbors to the south. Back in the late 80's, or very early 90's, I saw an interesting show on PBS. Robert Reich, a noted economist before he was the Labor Secretary for the Clinton administration, hosted this program. However, this was before anyone outside of Arkansas had heard of Clinton, or had any idea that Reich was even a Democrat. I know that I was crestfallen when I later found out that not only was he a Democrat, but that he was going to work for President Clinton.

Anyway, in this program Robert Reich had a demonstration showing how a healthy, stable economy acts. He placed a number of occupied chairs in a circle, and each of the people in the chairs started out with just a few dollars in their hand.

Then he had them each pass a dollar to their right every 10 seconds or so, to represent the money that they were spending on rent, food, mortgage, etc. The money that they received from the left represented their wages from work, or profits from their local business. So far--so good, everyone was making money and the economy was stable. Then he said that if you export goods--money from the outside starts to come into the economy. So now he introduced another dollar into the circle every few seconds. This resulted in growth for everyone. At any instant in time, every person had more dollars in his hand than when he started, and it was growing. Life was good. Then he demonstrated something else. He said that if you started to import more than you export, or spend your money with entities that do not live in the local community (thus, they do not spend their money in the local economy) something else happens. He then stopped introducing a dollar every few seconds, but started taking out a dollar every few seconds. Guess what? Right! Pretty soon everyone was broke. And you know what he called that community? A Ghetto. No middle class. Just poor. The rich live elsewhere.

The huge illegal alien community in this country sends, every week, hundreds of millions of dollars to their own home countries. That is money that goes out of circulation in this country and is not spent here, reducing the buying power of our citizens and resulting in less need for goods, services, and jobs. Don't mistake this as connecting the word ghetto and Mexican. A ghetto, as I am using the term, is a place of concentrated poor regardless of race or background. I have lived in a mixed-race neighborhood and enjoyed all my neighbors who were of many different races and nationalities. I just don't want to see this country turned into an economic ghetto.

Illegal immigration is not the sole cause of the ghettoizing of America. The other is the practice of outsourcing of jobs to countries with a lower labor cost. But, you know what? The dynamics of one is identical to the other; however, the outsourcing of jobs may even be worse because not only are you sending money out of the community in the form of wages, but you are sending more money out because of the need to increase imports to replace the lost local production. That is how ghettos are formed. That is also what has happened to Detroit, and what is currently happening on a larger scale to this entire country, and to every other developed country in the world. All because of the desire for business to chase "cheap labor" for the short term gain.

Henry Ford understood how to make this country great. When asked by his fellow automobile barons why he was willing to pay his workers (what was at the time) so much more than he (or they) had to. He replied, *"How else would they be able to afford to buy my cars?"* Or at least they were words to that effect. He was responsible for the rise of the middle class in this country, and indeed, was a model for all the developed countries in the world. Not because of his development of modern manufacturing methods (which certainly didn't hurt), but it was his insistence on giving his workers a good wage. A rising tide floats all boats.

What he did was create a large and affluent middle class. Check it out.

With that in mind, here is something for you to ponder:

1. A country's political stability is proportional to the size of its affluent middle class. That is, the larger the middle class is, the more politically stable a society is, and the result is that there is less likelihood of revolution. It makes sense; the more affluent (and happy) middle class people there are--the fewer pissed-off people there are. And it's the pissed-off people that the wealthy have to worry about; they're the ones who revolt.

2. The middle class in America has been shrinking for more than 30 years. It has been an ongoing struggle throughout history, in all societies, to get the wealthy and powerful to allow a middle class to grow and thrive; it encroaches on

their self ordained territory. That is why, until now, all societies (sooner or later) either disappear or suffer civil war or revolution. The wealthy, as a group, are blind and deaf to what goes on around them because of natural greed.

Think about that.

The American public has been a cash cow for business, and in the interest of increased profits for the companies who are outsourcing jobs or employing illegal aliens--the companies have stopped feeding the cow. It is inevitable; the cow is starving, and pretty soon the cow will die. 40% of this country's GDP is derived from consumer spending, and the short-sidedness and greed of many of our business and political leaders is impoverishing the consumer, and putting consumer spending in danger in order to fatten their pockets in the short term.

Henry Ford didn't chase lower wages; he increased wages. He knew that in order to milk the cash cow--you have to feed that same cash cow and keep it healthy. He was far sighted, and he understood that a large prosperous middle class was good for everyone. I repeat, "A rising tide floats all ships".

As a result Ford became one of the most rich and powerful of all the industrialists in history, and his company is one of the very few companies that have remained essentially unscathed after nearly 100 years.

Most people who are in power in business or government are not so far-sighted. As I also mentioned in an earlier post, when Lenin was asked to define a capitalist, he said, *"A capitalist is a man who will sell you the rope that you are going to hang him with."* In other words, it's all about increased profits now--the hell with later; I'll make my money now, and take care of later--later. You can't get any more short-sighted than that. Now I don't mean to paint all capitalists with the same broad brush. Most capitalists use their moral base, and good sense, while working within our economic system. But to some--capitalism is like a religion; it is supreme and everything else is secondary to making maximum profit--now. We always need to watch these people, and restrain them for their own good as well as ours. They remind me of an old illustration I once saw of a voracious snake swallowing its own tail.

Let's put a stop to the turning of this great country into a ghetto!

The first step is to button down our southern border, and enforce our immigration limits and laws. A reasonable immigration limit is fine and even desirable. But to continue to allow us to be inundated with cheap labor is to invite escalating fiscal disaster, or worse.

The second step is to hammer business people who hire illegal aliens, and I mean **hammer them hard**. We have laws on the books to fine those businesses so much per day for each illegal worker that they employ, but the government (both Republican and Democrat) has chosen to not enforce those laws. If you fine any company that employs illegal aliens--lets say--$500 per day--per illegal alien, and also charge any management who knowingly employs those same illegal aliens with a criminal violation that results in a fine and / or imprisonment, the job market for illegal aliens would disappear in an instant, and the job availability for legal residents, with appropriate wages, would grow just as fast. And what would be the result of that? Why, it would result in decreased unemployment, decreased welfare, and a growing middle class with more money in our pockets. Boy, that would sure suck--huh! Of course, we would also need more jail space for everyone in management in the meatpacking, and construction industries; but, of course, that too would create more jobs for jailors and lawyers.

If we were to round up all the illegal immigrants and send them back south of the border it wouldn't be the first time. There is, indeed, precedence. President Hoover, during the Great Depression, rounded up millions of Mexicans and sent them back to Mexico in order to give the work back to our own legal residents and citizens. Then, later, President Truman rounded up about 12 million Mexicans under 'Operation Wet Back' (that's not a joke, and not my words--look it up), and sent them packing in order to give returning WWII GI's jobs.

Notice the recurring theme? The Mexicans are a constant and continuing problem regarding the undermining of our own citizens' labor.

Regarding the increasing outsourcing of jobs the solution is simple; CONGRESS SHOULD PASS A LAW that requires anything that is sold here--to be manufactured here--period. Import (duty-free) only raw materials. Any other importation of anything, including sub-assemblies, would have to be offset by exports with an equal corresponding labor content, or pay a duty equal to the labor content, so as to pay for the resulting unemployment.

This will, indeed, cause or force other countries to pass similar laws to protect their own citizens. Great! The result will then (finally) be a truly level playing field in a still free-market. It just eliminates the exploitation of the labor of some countries at the expense of the citizenry of the developed countries by the current chasing of cheap labor; which we all know is exactly what our self-absorbed business and political leaders do not want. Protectionism isn't necessarily bad; the absence of protection inherently invites thieves. I'll just bet that if we were to pass such a law then Mexico would do it too, and then their citizens would have no need to come here to better themselves. **A rising tide floats all boats.**

I was now going to repeat the paragraph about *"to protect and to serve-Everyone"*, but I think I've made my point. It will not be repeated again. No sense beating a dead horse.

If you have made it this far you are probably an open-minded moderate. However, you could also just be a tolerant a**h***, which is really quite rare. This next post is about religion (in this country), in general, and Christianity in particular. Don't worry, it offers no opinions as to the validity or truth of **any** religion. However, continue only if you have an open mind.

Chapter 14

Are We A Christian Nation, Or A Nation Of Christians?

This week, being from Texas, one bit that was repeated on the news every day was a video of one of our U.S. Representatives (Gomert, if I remember right) ranting about a court ruling that stopped the government from authorizing an official "day of prayer".

What ticked me off were the two statements he issued. The first was that "we are a Christian nation", and the second was that this was another example of "legislating from the bench." You expect that kind of rhetoric from TV preachers like Pat Robertson. In fact, I have heard both opinions come out of the mouth of Pat Robertson, and many other preachers (and their followers). But, when I hear it from preachers it doesn't upset me at all. The duty to spread a religion (and convert those who believe otherwise) is the duty of all the true believers of essentially nearly all religions. You expect the staunchly religious to do just that because it is their religious duty. However, what does upset me is that an elected representative would suspend reason, logic, facts and the Constitution that protects us all--in order to either try to force his own religious beliefs on the rest of us, or to pander to a vocal group that supports him.

I do not have the ability to read his mind, but it doesn't matter (it's probably like reading a blank page). An elected representative should make every effort to be correct (or, at least, accurate) in his public opinion, and represent and protect everyone.

First lets look at the "legislating from the bench" comment. The first amendment to the Constitution is about guaranteeing the freedom of religion. This has been interpreted as meaning anyone is free to believe in any religion they wish, including not believing in any religion at all. It has also been interpreted to mean that the U.S. government will **not sponsor any religion at all**. This has been the accepted interpretation from day one. If the government were to authorize a "national day of prayer" it would, in fact, be sponsoring religions that are founded in a belief in a God or gods, and the desirability in praying to them. **This** is clearly not allowed in the U.S. Constitution. So, how is it that a judge who rules that the government can't authorize a "national day of prayer", is "legislating from the bench". That is an irrational supposition. If the judge had ruled otherwise, that, indeed, would have been legislating from the bench. The second statement that this is "a Christian Nation" is also erroneous. To be a Christian Nation would not just mean that the nation was built on Christian values, but also would mean that our nation MUST not only support, but also promote and enforce one or more of the various Christian sects to the exclusion of all other religious beliefs. You may still be tolerant of other religious beliefs to some extent, but a Christian Nation would be **required** to have laws based on the "official" Christian religion, much like how Israel's laws are based on the Jewish religion, Iran's laws are based on the Islamic religion, and so forth. That would be great for hard core Christians, but it sure would suck for everyone else. Keep in mind that whenever the Christians were in control of governments in the past, bloodshed followed. First there were the Crusades. Then there was the Spanish Inquisition and Auto de fe'. Lets not forget the Salem Witch Trials. And even as late as the 1800's, the Mormon Church (they are Christian too), who were hounded out of the eastern states, was said to be pretty intolerant of other beliefs, and were rumored to be pretty bloody effective at stifling dissent and getting revenge (the rumored Danites). That's why our Constitution has a first amendment, and it has been interpreted to mean that anyone can believe in anything, or they can believe in nothing, and the government will not take sides.

You also hear as proof that we are a Christian Nation by the inclusion of *"In God We Trust"* on our currency, and the mention of God in various documents and on government buildings. While this inclusion is true--think back to 1790 when this Constitution was written. That was only 98 years after the Salem Witch Trials where they burned supposed heretics at the stake, and tortured or drowned them. Simply acknowledging freedom of (and freedom from) religion was a big leap for our founding fathers. The overwhelmingly dominant religion at the time was, indeed, the various Christian sects (most of whom were themselves hounded out of Europe during and after the Reformation), so it's easy to understand the inclusion of "God" into their various writings and instruments of government. By the way, the words *"under God"* wasn't added to the Pledge of Allegiance until the mid-fifties after the fear of Senator McCarthy got everyone falling all over themselves to prove that they were not godless commies. But notice that, unless I am mistaken, there is little or no mention of "Jesus" or "Christ" in official documents, just God. That shows that they were not promoting Christianity. Does that mean the opposite? Is this country, then, really a Jewish or Muslim nation? No, not at all.

You must also remember that, at the time of our founding, nearly everyone believed in some kind of religion. It was an extremely courageous (and rare) person who would publicly proclaim no belief in any religion.

The Holy Bible even supports the separation of Church and State. Didn't Jesus say to render unto Caesar that which is

Caesars', and render unto God that which is Gods'? Since Jesus admitted to talking almost exclusively in parables it is reasonable to not interpret this narrowly (referring only to money), but you could interpret that verse as advocating the separation of Church and State. In fact, the Roman government didn't even want to try or punish Jesus, but bowed to the wishes of the local Church. How's that for Church influence. Nowhere in the Bible does anything mention that the Christian religion should dominate a nation.

This is not, then, a Christian Nation, but rather a Nation that is made up of a very large but shrinking percentage of Christians. A nation that, as a result, promotes Christian values, but does not promote the Christian religion so as to be inclusive to everyone, and as a result treats everyone equally and fairly.

One thing to keep in mind, when discussing the Constitution's position on any particular issue, is the one thing that nearly all of us forget; but fortunately our Judges do not forget to consult it. That is the Preamble To The Constitution. This is more than just a bunch of pretty words. It is the guiding light that judges use when deciding something that isn't specifically mentioned in the Constitution.

"We the People of the United States, in Order to form a more perfect Union, establish Justice, insure domestic Tranquility, provide for the Common defense, promote the general welfare, and secure the Blessings of Liberty to ourselves and our

Posterity, do ordain and establish this Constitution for the United States of America."

This allows (and mandates) latitude when deciding on issues that can help or hurt any portions of our people. As I mentioned earlier in this rant, I do not mind hearing pro-religious rants from clergy. That is their job and calling. I do not, however, like to hear it from our elected representatives who are supposed to keep the Constitution always in mind. Their job, and calling, is to represent and protect **EVERYONE**. Any politician who publicly denounces judges who are correctly following the Constitution, or pushes the opinion that a particular religion should have a favored status, is either a narrow-minded nut job, or is subverting his honest opinion in order to pander to a specific constituency; they are either stupid, or corrupt. In either case, he or she should be replaced at the first opportunity.

The following was added in 2012.

I think that now is a good time to make something clear. I am not an Atheist--I do not believe that there is no God, but I also do not believe everything that is preached in organized religion; there is just too much conflicting things in the Bible.

In the sincere hope that there is, indeed, an afterlife and a supreme being that rewards those who are good--I behave and try to treat everyone well, or at least, not harm them. But as you have probably already noticed by now, I refuse to follow others blindly (faith).

Hey, I'm not done yet!

Just kidding! As Porky Pig would say, "th-th, th-that's all folks."

P.S. Oh, yeah! In the unlikely event that you haven't learned anything new (as I promised at the beginning of the book), here is an interesting side note about the Destroyer that I served on in the U.S. Navy. The **U.S.S. Theodore E. Chandler DD717** was named after a WWII Admiral named Theodore E. Chandler who was killed in a Japanese kamikaze attack. Big deal--you say. And now (as the late Paul Harvey would say) for the rest of the story. What is really interesting is that this same Admiral Theodore E. Chandler was a great grandson of a lady who was the fiancée of John Wilkes Booth, and who also was two-timing Booth with Robert Todd Lincoln (Abe's son) just prior to the assassination of President Lincoln. Wow! I just recently learned that useless tidbit. Wait a second! I just used it so it must not be all that useless. Some of you may have known about Booth's two-timing fiancé, and some of you may have known about my Destroyer and the Admiral it was named after, but I'll bet not many of you knew the whole story. **My earlier promise of enlightenment is fulfilled.**

****

The end...Really!!

Authors email address is: lmarxsen@yahoo.com

Blog is at: http://insearchofcompetence.blogspot.com

www.ingramcontent.com/pod-product-compliance
Lightning Source LLC
Chambersburg PA
CBHW051456170526
45166CB00001B/270